Fighting The Amalekites*
Second Edition

A Guide to Spiritual Warfare

*am'- a- lek – ite — (1) enemy that ambushes; (2) habit that insults the sacred; (3) adversary of the weak; (4) evil that destroys.

Hollis L. Green, ThD, PhD

AN IMPRINT OF
GLOBALEDADVANCEPRESS

FIGHTING THE AMALEKITES* Second Edition

A Guide to Spiritual Warfare

Copyright © 2014 by Hollis L. Green

Library of Congress Control Number: 2014931180

ISBN 978-1-935434-30-6

Subject Codes and Description: 1: REL 012000: Religion: Christian Life - General 2: REL 012040: Religion: Christian Life - Inspirational 3: REL 012070: Religion: Christian Life - Personal Growth

All rights reserved, including the right to reproduce this book or any part thereof in any form, except for inclusion of brief quotations in a review, without the written permission of the author and GlobalEdAdvance Press.

Cover Design by Global Graphics

Author photo by Carie Burchfield-Ofori cariephoto@gmail.com

Printed in Australia, Brazil, France, Germany, Italy, Spain, UK, and USA.

The Press does not have ownership of the contents of a book; this is the author's work and the author owns the copyright. All theory, concepts, constructs, and perspectives are those of the author and not necessarily the Press. They are presented for open and free discussion of the issues involved. All comments and feedback should be directed to the Email: [comments4author@aol.com] and the comments will be forwarded to the author for response.

Published by
PostGutenberg Books™
an imprint of
GlobalEdAdvance Press
www.gea-books.com

Dedication

Remembering his courage to take the Love of Christ outside the four walls of the Church, this book is dedicated to

Chaplain Robert D. Crick, U.S. Army (Ret.)

With respect for his 21 years of active service as Chaplain in the U.S. Army with service in Vietnam. His wartime service was recognized with the Legion of Merit, Bronze Star with two Oak Leaf Clusters for Valor, and several other notable commendations and decorations.

Organized religion will never prevail over the basic evil that plagues the world. Spiritual warfare is normally an offensive waged by believers who are alone. It is guerilla warfare behind the lines with individual believers working as a lone sniper zeroing in on current evil practices that become besetting sins. These personal battles are not limited to the young, the struggle is a lifestyle offensive. Where organized groups choose not to function, personal action is required to make a real difference and break down the barriers to spiritual progress. There are no surrogate warriors, each individual must fight their own personal battles in order to grow in grace and spiritual knowledge. Surely, there are processes and practices that groups may perform that can assist individuals to combat evil forces; however, each person must fight their own spiritual battles. Those who overcome and prevail against evil have special divine promises:

> 7. He that overcomes shall inherit these things; and I will be his God, and he shall be My son. 8. But the cowards, the unbelieving, the defiled, and murderers, and fornicators, and those who claim magical powers, and the worshiper of idols, and all teller of lies, will have their part in the lake that burns with fire and brimstone: which is the second death. (Revelation 21:7, 8 EDNT)

Table Of Contents

INTRODUCTION — 9

CHAPTER ONE
TILL EVERY FOE IS VANQUISHED — 21

CHAPTER TWO
A WORLD IN SPIRITUAL DARKNESS — 29

CHAPTER THREE
A STRATEGY AGAINST STRONGHOLDS — 41

CHAPTER FOUR
KINDRED MINDS JOINED IN HEART — 55

CHAPTER FIVE
ARMED WITH WATCHFUL CARE — 75

CHAPTER SIX
STORMING THE RAMPARTS — 89

CHAPTER SEVEN
SOLDIERS OF THE CROSS — 105

CHAPTER EIGHT
A BULWARK NEVER FAILING — 117

AFTERWORD — 129

APPENDIX
SPIRITUAL COMBAT RESOURCES — 135

A CROWNING ACHIEVEMENT — 141

am'- a - lek - ite — (1) enemy that ambushes; (2) habit that insults the sacred; (3) adversary of the weak; (4) evil that destroys.

Introduction

History of the Amalekites

The Amalekites attacked the Israelites without apparent provocation during the Exodus from Egypt (Exodus 17:8).

> Remember what the Amalekites did to you along the way when you came out of Egypt. When you were weary and worn out, they met you on your journey and cut off all who were lagging behind; they had no fear of God. When the Lord your God gives you rest from all the enemies around you in the land he is giving you to possess as an inheritance, you shall blot out the memory of Amalek from under heaven. Do not forget! (Deuteronomy 25:17-19 NIV)

They later attacked Israel during the time of the Judges and often raided the land after the Israelites had planted crops, leaving them with nothing. God ordered Saul to utterly destroy everything related to the Amalekites:

> Samuel said to Saul, "I am the one the Lord sent to anoint you king over his people Israel; so listen now to the message from the Lord. This is what the Lord Almighty says: 'I will punish the Amalekites for what they did to Israel when they waylaid them as they came up from Egypt. Now go, attack the Amalekites and totally destroy everything that belongs to them. Do not spare them; put to death men and women, children and infants, cattle and sheep, camels and donkeys. (1 Samuel 15:1-3 NIV)

This was over 300 years after the Amalekites first attacked Israel. They continuously raided and plundered other cities up to the time of Saul and David. The Amalekites that Saul and David warred against were clearly no better than their ancestors who had first waylaid Israel. The Amalekites could have been totally destroyed by Saul (1 Samuel 15) had he followed God's instructions. He did destroy the city of Amalek, but other raiding parties/nomadic bands of Amalekites survived. These were defeated by David (1 Samuel 30) with the exception of a few hundred who escaped. At least one survived to finish off Saul, and it appears a few Amalekites remain in the modern world. The "little Amalekites" still plague and pester all who attempt a faith-based lifestyle. The spiritual battle against the Amalekites continues.

"Fighting the Amalekites" was a topic used in my early ministry with young people. It dealt with the habits, weaknesses and transgressions that hinder spiritual progress. The foundation of the message was how the Amalekites ambushed Israel coming out of Egypt and Saul's failure to obey the clear command "Utterly destroy the work of the Amalekites." Habits that insult the sacred and disobedient behavior are "spiritual Amalekites" waiting to ambush believers. When one fails to destroy these things, they will ultimately bring personal destruction. This is what happened to King Saul: an Amalekite finished him off after he fatally wounded himself.

After the battle went against Saul and his sons and servants were dead, Saul attempted suicide by falling on his sword. While his enemies were approaching fast, Saul still alive turned to see a young man and asked, "Who are you?" The answer, "I am an Amalekite," must have been an arrow piercing his disobedient heart. Saul told the young Amalekite, "Come stand upon me and slay me, for my life is yet whole in me." The cost of Saul's failure to destroy the Amalekites was the loss of not only his life but the lives of many warriors, including his sons and servants. Elements of his incomplete obedience to destroy the Amalekites were present at his downfall and completed his destruction. The Amalekite took his Crown, the symbol of God's anointing and his power and influence with the people. (2 Samuel 1:5-10)

The Amalekites were an ancient and nomadic marauding people who usually sided with the enemies of God's People. Moses felt the wrath of an unprovoked attack on the Israelites for which God decreed continual war and ultimate obliteration. (Exodus 17:8ff) Amalek in an ambush attached the "hindmost" of the Israelite troop coming out of Egypt, "even all that were feeble behind thee, when thou wast faint and weary; and he feared not God." Israel was told to blot out the remembrance of Amalek from under heaven, and God warned "thou shalt not forget it." Joshua and the spies encountered the Amalekites in Canaan where the Amalekites together with the Canaanites overcame Israel. (Deuteronomy 25:18, 19).

During the period of the Judges, the Amalekites sided with the Ammonites and Moabites against the Israelites and with the Midianites against Gideon. Saul was told to utterly destroy the Amalekites for their animosity and ambush against the Israelites, but failed in this important mission and after Saul's sons were killed in battle and Saul's attempt to take his own life failed; it was an Amalekite who came and finished the task and took Saul's crown to David. It was King David who later subdued the Amalekites. (2 Samuel 1:1f)

Who will Fight the Amalekites?

One must lay aside every weight and sin that so easily overwhelms. Addictions that control must be conquered. Bad habits that destroy your testimony must be broken. Vocabulary that does not honor God must be replaced. Protect the health of your body and mind. These are the little "amalekites" that ambush you and take advantage of your weaknesses. Believers must always be on the alert and ready to defend themselves and others from evil forces. Remember the old adage: "An ounce of prevention is worth a pound of cure!" Destroying the "amalekites" in your life is necessary for full obedience and a testimony worthy of the price of redemption.

Avoidance is easier than recuperation and recovery. Another old adage speaks loudly to this issue: "A bird with a broken wing never flies as high!" If cleanliness is next to godliness, then prevention is akin to holiness. To separate from evil, to remain free from the normal sins of the human race, and to build a life of Christian living requires the assistance of the Holy Spirit and complete obedience to the Captain of our Salvation: Jesus Christ. The things that hinder your spiritual progress are "little amalekites" and are bold against all good because they fear not God. Cromwell, an early English churchman, had a motto written on his pocket Bible in Latin—*qui cessat esse melior cessat esse bonus*—"he who ceases to be better ceases to be good." Bad habits are easy to pick up, but difficult to put down. In fact, it takes about 21 days to break a bad habit by substituting another activity or behavior; but only one slip and the habit is back stronger than before. Remember the scripture about the devil returning and finding the house cleaned; seven more devils moved into the house. The latter end was worse that the beginning. (Luke 11:24-26) Care must be taken when dealing with the "bad stuff" the little amalekites; assistance and guidance are needed. Vigilance is required. Perseverance is necessary. Spiritual boldness is helpful. Putting on the whole armor of the Spirit is the best shield against the return of the "things" that pull you down.

Unproductive behavior, unhealthy habits, and failure to follow spiritual guidance, are the little "Amalekites" that ambush believers and take advantage of their weaknesses. All believers must be on alert, every ready to defend themselves and others from the deceitful forces of evil. Remembering the adage "An ounce of prevention is worth a pound of cure," could make believers aware of the "Amalekites" that may ambush them on their spiritual journey. Believers must arm themselves with the full armor of God and be ready for the conflict and the struggle of spiritual warfare.

Little Foxes or Amalekites

In the foxhunts of the English countryside, all are eager, men, horses, and dogs to find the fox. In an effort to catch a full-grown fox, they jump ditches, wade streams, leap over walls and hedges. Meanwhile, there is little energy used to remove the Amalekites that ambush believers on their journey. What about the little foxes ready to spoil the vineyard? Consider the lack of concern for the weights and sins that easily overwhelm believers every day. What about the Amalekites hiding in the darkness ready to pounce on the unsuspected?

The process to search and destroy the "little Amalekites" that may eventually disgrace and/or destroy you and your family is two-fold: prayer and patience. There must be a sincere desire to rid your life of the enemies that ambush your witness. One must remember that the basic human condition militates against progress in the spiritual life. A life of faith requires a state of endurance under difficult circumstances to arrive at true spiritual maturity. The body is in conflict with the Spirit and believers must side with the Spirit in persistent prayer to maintain a state of victory. Prayer and patience are the weapons to rid the faith-based life of the Amalekites that are waiting in ambush along the way.

Be vigilant! The intent of this book is to show that the Amalekites in one's life must be "utterly destroyed" or just as King Saul, they will return in time of trouble to bring personal destruction. They will take your crown, remove your identity, and leave you on the spiritual battlefield for the scavengers.

An Effort to Rally the Troops

A philosophical dichotomy has developed between how a person sees himself/herself and how a person behaves. The eyes of ethical leaders have become accustomed to the moral darkness and their minds blinded to the light of truth. Without moral leadership, the public has grown soft on sin, accepting personal sins, even in public places, as an unalienable right. These "cherished sins" speak loudly to the youth: "What I do does not affect who I am!" This construct is certainly not verifiable by Holy Scripture. Although a few aspects of systematic theology may be misconstrued to suggest that one may live anyway he/she pleases just because once upon a time they accepted Christ's forgiveness, this is far from orthodox teaching and is a dangerous concept.

General Good Suffers

The general good suffers when one is not accountable for private behavior. Jesus called this the "leaven of the Pharisees. Scripture declared that secret sins would be made public and that gossip whispered in the closet would be shouted from the housetop. With hidden sin to be ultimately uncovered, why does anyone persist in a life of immorality? What you fail to destroy may well destroy you!

> Never distess the Holy Spirit of God, whereby you have been marked for the day of redemption. (Ephesians 4:30 EDNT)

Victory is Lost

Spiritual victory is normally lost because of a fear of confrontation. Is the spirit of the Biblical Prophet dead and buried? Is there no one to say to the King, "Thou art the man?" Not only do evil forces assault individual Christians, there seems to be an all out warfare against

Christian ethics and faith-based morality, or anything that hints at the essential elements of a Christian Heritage. Is nothing sacred? What is next: "In God we trust" on the coins or "Under God" in the Pledge of Allegiance? All who would live the Christian life or become leaders for the Christian cause must resist evil forces or ultimate victory is surely lost. When one stumbles and brings disgrace to the Christian cause, all believers suffer the stigma of insincerity. Again, where is the spirit of the Biblical Prophet that declares there is sin in the camp?

Disgrace through Immorality

As one good leader after another falls in disgrace through immorality, it is time to declare war on the forces of Satan and stand in the gap and pray. Leaders must have clean and upright living to validate the message of God's saving grace. People will not drink from a contaminated well. They will not listen to a false prophet in the ministry for the money. The people will not long follow a political leader who does not demonstrate a moral and ethical foundation. The Christian life must be lived in power and glory for the world to see the value of walking with God.

A Strategic Resistance

Believers must organize a strategic resistance to all things evil:
- live the resurrected life and walk in the Spirit to demonstrate that Satan has no power over us or the work that God has called us to do.
- make a new and fresh commitment to right living in order to protect the witness of the saints and the message of the gospel.
- join the over-comers and enlist in the battle to behave what they believe.

Moral leaders must rally the troops at a personal level and develop a strategy of resistance; however, the most potent weapons are:
- personal prayer and
- the guidance of the Holy Spirit.

The Congregation ought to stand ready to act responsibly. Believers must work together as saints triumphant!

Gilboa - a Place of Triumph and Tragedy

According to Jewish History, Mt. Gilboa is a place of tragedy and triumph. Gilboa was the site of Gideon's great victory over the Midianites and the Amalekites. Yet, it was at Gilboa that Saul, the first King of Israel, and his sons died fighting the Philistines, "And it came to pass on the morrow, when the Philistines came to strip the slain, that they found Saul and his three sons fallen in mount Gilboa" (1 Samuel 38:8). King David, who replaced Saul, lamented his fallen king and cursed the place "Ye mountains of Gilboa, let there be no dew, neither let there be rain, upon you, nor fields of offerings: for there the shield of the mighty is vilely cast away, the shield of Saul, as though he had not been anointed with oil." (II Samuel

1:21 KJV) Over the years – some have taken this curse literally, as the reason for the baldness of Mt. Gilboa. However, in recent years Jewish funds have planted thousands of trees and greatly changed the appearance of Gilboa, although bald spots are still clearly visible.

Gilboa is now a popular scenic place from February to April for picnics among the multitude of wildflowers and the purplish Gilboa Iris. How soon humanity forgets both the triumph and tragedy of the site. Does this not bring to memory the repaired veil in the Temple after it was "rent in two from the top to the bottom" at the death of Jesus. The open veil was to provide an unencumbered access to the Holy Place, but the system soon reverted to the old ways. Now, the planting of trees on Gilboa is an attempt to overcome the curse of King David. Be it known to all: your sins will find you out. Whether it is the sin of Achan hiding stolen things in his tent, or the greed of Ananias and Sapphira who lied to the Holy Spirit in holding back promised funds. The perpetrator of wrong deeds will always be punished.

Gilboa - a Place of Triumph

Gilboa, a significant place in Israel's military history, where the Lord instructed Gideon to reduce his forces so that it would be obvious that God was responsible for the victory against the Midianites and Amalekites. Gideon obeyed the Lord and Gideon's tiny band of 300 routed the enemy (Judges 7:1-25) and God received the credit. Gideon's obedience brought victory in one of the most remarkable conflicts of Israel's history.

Gilboa - a Place of Tragedy

It was also at Gilboa that Saul's disobedience in failing to utterly destroy the Amalekites was finally punished. After the battle was lost and Saul attempted suicide, an

Amalekite came on the scene. Saul asked him to finish the botched job of suicide so he would not fall into the hands of the enemy alive. It was an Amalekite who stood upon Saul's dying body and made the final strike that finished Saul. It was an Amalekite that took Saul's crown. Saul's disobedience of not utterly destroying all the Amalekites returned to finish Saul. **The things he failed to destroy, in the end destroyed him**. This should be a lesson to all. (2 Samuel 1:4-13 KJV)

> 4 And David said unto him, How went the matter? I pray thee, tell me. And he answered, That the people are fled from the battle, and many of the people also are fallen and dead; and Saul and Jonathan his son are dead also. 5 And David said unto the young man that told him, How knowest thou that Saul and Jonathan his son be dead? 6 And the young man that told him said, As I happened by chance upon mount Gilboa, behold, Saul leaned upon his spear; and, lo, the chariots and horsemen followed hard after him. 7 And when he looked behind him, he saw me, and called unto me. And I answered, Here am I. 8 And he said unto me, Who art thou? And I answered him, I am an Amalekite. 9 And he said unto me again, Stand, I pray thee, upon me, and slay me: for anguish is come upon me, because my life is yet whole in me. 10 So I stood upon him, and slew him, because I was sure that he could not live after that he was fallen: and I took the crown that was upon his head, and the bracelet that was on his arm, and have brought them hither unto my lord. 11 Then David took hold on his clothes, and rent them; and likewise all the men that were with him: 12 And they mourned, and wept, and fasted until even, for Saul, and for Jonathan his son, and for the people of the Lord, and for the house of Israel; because they were fallen by the sword. 13 And David said unto the young man that told him, Whence art thou? And he answered, I am the son of a stranger, an Amalekite. (2 Samuel 1:4-13 KJV)

New Testament scriptures are from
The EVERGREEN Devotional New Testament (EDNT)

(Print or eBook available at www.gea-books.com or anywhere good books are sold)

CHAPTER ONE
Till Every Foe Is Vanquished

>Stand up, stand up for Jesus,
>Ye soldiers of the cross;
>Lift high His royal banner,
>It must not suffer loss: vict'ry unto vict'ry
>His army shall He lead,
>Till every foe is vanquished
>And Christ is Lord indeed.
>
>- George Duffield, Jr.-

God Leaves a Lot of Work for Us

My paternal grandfather was a faithful Methodist who believed and trusted God. He was primarily a farmer and one year showed a distinguished crop of corn to a city visitor. The fellow thought grandfather was too proud of his own labors and told him to be grateful to God for providing the land, the sunshine, the rain, and in reality it was God who made the corn grow. After listening to the exhortation, grandfather retaliated; "I know God is working, but you should have seen that field when God had it by Himself! He sure left a lot of work for me to do."

God is working and has the power to do all the work, but leaves a great deal to us. The Scripture affirms "God is working, and we are together." The task of the Congregation is to get together: "one mind, one place, one accord." Each believer must make a commitment to the work at hand. The Believer cannot depend on God to come down from His Throne and fight the evil in the world. In fact, God has done all He needs to do: He gave his Son! Jesus gave His life and the Holy Spirit is present in the world to convict of sin, righteousness, and judgment. The Spirit is also present to equip, empower, protect, and guide believers in the work that needs to be done. On the other hand, Christians must be willing to obey and follow God's clear commands.

Bold Action to Destroy the Enemy

Amalek ambushed the Children of Israel as they came out of Egypt. He attacked the rear of the marching column where the feeble were at the end of a long day when all were faint and weary. God instructed Israel that after they had rested from all their enemies in the land that they should blot out the remembrance of Amalek. They were warned not to forget it.

The First Battle

Moses ordered Joshua to select and organize the men for their first real battle. Moses was to go to the top of a hill and hold up his hands and Joshua and the warriors were to attack Amalek. As long as Moses held up his hands, Joshua prevailed, but when Moses dropped his hands, Amalek prevailed. Aaron and Hur found a stone for Moses to sit on and with one on each side they held up the hands of Moses until the sun went down. Joshua disconcerted and defeated Amalek and his army, but did not vanquish everyone. Moses rehearsed God's wish for the complete destruction of Amalek and built an altar and said, "The Lord will have war with Amalek from generation to generation." (Exodus 17:8-16) Amalek continued to wage guerrilla warfare against Israel. Moses rehearsed God's wish for the complete destruction of Amalek and built an altar and said, "The Lord will have war with Amalek from generation to generation." (Exodus 17:8-16) Amalek continued to wage guerrilla warfare against Israel. The first battle required teamwork and a together-strong mindset; each and every battle until the last one will require people working together. The wise man Solomon said clearly:

> Two are better than one; because they have a good reward for their labour. For if they fall, the one will lift up his fellow: but woe to him that is alone when he falleth; for he hath not another to help him up. (Ecclesiastes 4:9-10)

King Saul Failed

After Saul was made King, he was ordered to go to battle against Amalek:

> Thus saith the Lord of hosts, I remember that which Amalek did to Israel, how he laid wait for him in the way, when he came up from Egypt. Now go and smite Amalek, and utterly destroy all that they have, and spare them not; but slay both man and woman, infant and suckling, ox and sheep, camel and ass. And Saul smote the Amalekites and utterly destroyed all the people, but spared Agag, and the best of the sheep, oxen, fatlings, and lambs. (1 Samuel 15:2-3)

God intended that every foe be vanquished and even the memory of the Amalekites be blotted out of history, but Saul failed to carry out this mission. Saul was rejected as King because of disobedience and later an Amalekite, a remnant of his disobedience, actually put an end to both Saul's kingdom and his life.

The Battle went Against Saul

The Philistines fought against Israel continually. As King Saul and his sons were in their last battle, his sons were killed and Saul was wounded. Saul asked his armor bearer to kill him to avoid capture by the Philistines, but he refused. Saul then attempted to kill himself by falling on his sword. Thinking Saul to be dead, his armor bearer died with him. Although mortally wounded, Saul was not dead.

Learning of the defeat of Saul, David went to battle and slaughtered the Amalekites. Three days after the battle, David learned that one Amalekite remained alive. The actual scripture reference tells the story best:

> 2 It came even to pass on the third day, that, behold, a man came out of the camp from Saul with his clothes rent, and earth upon his head: and so it was, when he came to David, that he fell to the earth, and did obeisance. 3 And David said unto him, From whence comest thou? And he said unto him, Out of the camp of Israel am I escaped. 4 And David said unto him, How went the matter? I pray thee, tell me. And he answered, That the people are fled from the battle, and many of the people also are fallen and dead; and Saul and Jonathan his son are dead also. 6 And David said unto the young man that told him, How knowest thou that Saul and Jonathan his son be dead? 6 And the young man that told him said, As I happened by chance up mount Gilboa, behold, Saul leaned upon his spear; and, lo, the chariots and horsemen followed hard after him. 7 And when he looked behind him, he saw me, and called unto me. And I answered, Here am I. 8 And he said unto me, Who art thou? And I answered him, I am an Amalekite. 9 He said unto me again, Stand, I pray thee, upon me, and slay me; for anguish is come upon me, because my life is yet whole in me. 10 So I stood upon him, and slew him, because I was sure that he could not live after that he was fallen; and I took the crown that was upon his head, and the bracelet that was on his arm, and have bought them hither unto my lord. (1 Samuel 31; 2 Samuel 1:1-10)

An Amalekite Finished Saul

The Amalekites that Saul failed to destroy through disobedience were present to finish Saul off after he had mortally wounded himself. The Amalekite stood upon Saul and thrust the sword deeper. He took Saul's crown and gave it to another. What irony. God said, "Utterly destroy the Amalekites!" Here in the moment of disgrace, when the battle was lost, when his sons were dead, when the kingdom was lost, it was an Amalekite that actually took Saul's crown. In the final moments of Saul's life, he must have been reminded of his disobedience. That which we fail to destroy through disobedience, God will use to destroy us in the end. This is why we must strongly resist evil until every foe of the Christian cause is vanquished.

God wants each of us to fight the good fight of faith until every enemy is defeated. All the evil we spare in our personal lives, in our families, in our congregations, or in the Nation will bring disgrace and dishonor in the end. We must resist evil until Christ is Lord indeed. All failure will return to haunt us at the point of disgrace and death.

Destroy your Amalekites

Christian Leadership has failed to deal adequately with the immoral Amalekites. A careless attitude toward evil can bring destruction. Unless the immoral Amalekites are utterly destroyed, Satan will continually use them to ambush and defeat the Christian testimony.

Attitude is a predisposition to act in a particular manner; consequently, attitude has a great deal to do with a believer's walk of faith and daily human relationships. It is the responsibility of each believer to develop an attitude of obedience and a resistance to evil. Scripture warns believers to bring into captivity every thought to the obedience of Christ.

> 3. Human beings we may be, but we do not fight our battles in human strength: 4. the weapons we use to fight are not human, but mighty through God to demolish strongholds; 5. casting down the conceits of men against the knowledge

of God, and bringing every human thought into obedience to Christ; 6. when your submission reaches completion, I am prepared to settle all scores with the disobedient. (2 Corinthians 10:3-6 EDNT)

Complete Obedience

The process of complete obedience is accomplished through an act of the will, the decision-making mechanism of the mind that consciously decides to submit to the control of the Holy Spirit. This conscious act of the will brings the attitude into positive focus so that one can call upon the power of the recreated spirit to adjust the mind and attitude until it is attuned to spiritual things. Paul expressed to the Ephesians a firm belief that all Christian attitudes and thoughts must be constantly changing for the better (Ephesians 4:23). The big questions are: How is this accomplished? How can the believer be renewed in the spirit of his mind? In a troubled world, how can a person develop a predisposition to obedience? This comes only with true repentance, spiritual regeneration of the soul, and a daily commitment to wage aggressive battle against the "amalekites" that wish to destroy both will and witness.

> ... and the spirit of your mind must be remade; and that you clothe yourself as a new man, which after God is created in righteousness and the holiness of truth. (Ephesians 4:23, 24 EDNT)

> 17. This I command solemnly in the Lord, that you henceforth behave not as Gentiles, in the arrogance of their mind, 18. having clouded powers of discernment, being estranged from the life of God, although ignorance prevails among them, because of the blindness of their heart: 19. having lost all sense of shame have given themselves over to sensuality, to practice all forms of immorality without restraint. 20. This is not the lesson you learned from Christ: 21. if you have

been instructed by Him and listened to the truth in Jesus. 22. For you learned concerning your former behavior, that the old man was corrupt according to deceitful passions; 23. and the spirit of your mind must be remade; 24. and that you clothe yourself as a new man, which after God is created in righteousness and the holiness of truth. 25. Wherefore speak every man truth with his neighbor without falsehood: for we are members bound one to another. 26. Have righteous anger without sin: let not the sun go down on your anger: 27. Neither give an opportunity to the devil. 28. The thief must steal no more, but let him do honest work with his hands, that he may have something to share with the needy. 29. Let no unwholesome words come from your mouth, but only good words for enriching, that it may serve as a blessing to the hearers. 30. Never distress the Holy Spirit of God, whereby you have been marked for the day of redemption. 31. Let your bitter frame of mind, anger and violent outbreak or brawling, and abusive language, be put away from you with all hatred: 32. Become gracious to one another, tenderly affectionate, ready to forgive one another, even as God for Christ's sake forgave you. (Ephesians 4:17-32 EDNT)

CHAPTER TWO
A World In Spiritual Darkness

And tho this world, with devils filled,
Should threaten to undo us,
We will not fear, for God hath willed,
His truth to triumph thru us.
The prince of darkness grim,
We tremble not for him
His rage we can endure,
For lo, his doom is sure;
One little word shall fell him: "Jesus"

- Martin Luther -

Saints Defined

Believers must resist evil and reclaim the sacred places for spiritual worship. Traveling in Peru gathering stories for a magazine, I arrived in Lima on the week the Pope declared that several Saints were to be taken off the official Vatican list. Searching the streets of Lima for someone who could speak English better than my Spanish, a young man about 25 was found and asked about the Pope's decision to take certain Saints off the list. He said it didn't matter, that the people could still pray to them, but the leaders just wouldn't teach the next generation to recognize them. I asked, "Why would you want to continue to pray to a Saint whom the Pope said was really not worthy?" He responded in effect that the idea of saints was to encourage people to pray, the power was not in the saint, but in the person praying. That was good reasoning, so I pushed the conversation, "What is a Saint, and why does the Church select them?"

He proceeded to explain that "a saint is someone who lives so well that they bypassed Purgatory and go straight to Heaven when they die."

According to that definition and my theology: my plans to by-pass purgatory on my way to heaven, I was a saint. Offering my hand and an introduction, "I am Saint Hollis!" He appeared frightened, but did not say a word. He just turned and walked away rapidly. After a few steps, he turned and took another look at me, a few more steps and turned again. I think he believed that I was one of the saints that had been taken off the list who had appeared to him. I observed as he continued toward a Church, where I assumed he would pray or tell his Priest about meeting Saint Hollis. On my next visit to Lima, there may well be a Shrine to Saint Hollis on that corner. If so, I will pause and thank God that He has provided a direct path for me to bypass Purgatory on my way to heaven. In scripture all true, faithful, soldiers of the Cross were considered saints and will have direct access to heaven.

As a follow-up on this story, I asked a little boy "What is your definition of a Saint?" He thought for a moment, and then eagerly said, "A Saint is someone the light shines through!' Further inquiry as to where he learned the definition. He said "My church has stain-glass windows with pictures of Saints and the light shine through them into the sanctuary every Sunday morning."

Soldiers, Faithful, True and Bold

Although discord is evident everywhere, many choose to ignore the obvious. Most are not aware of the present work of the Holy Spirit, who walks beside believers to protect and empower each one for the battle against evil. It is the Spirit that gives "boldness" (fluency of speech and action) to believers. Most do not see the

Angels of the Lord encamped about gathered believers ready to protect and empower them in their struggle against evil. The eyes of some have become accustomed to the lingering spiritual darkness that causes limited vision and creates a false sense of security; consequently, they are unaware of and unprepared for the attacks of Satan and his cohorts. Those faithful Christian soldiers who are true to the word will have the boldness of the Holy Spirit to guide their action against enemies of Christ.

From the traumatic moment of birth to the solid jolting of everyday life situations, human beings face a hostile world. Much of the hostility comes from a conflict between good and evil. The subtle clash between the evil forces of darkness and the light of spiritual truth is often seen as a normal part of human existence. Because of moral decadence, much of the world lives in the shadow of despair. The light of the Gospel is filtered through spiritual darkness. The corrupting forces of evil work beneath the surface of world order to discourage and discredit all who would live the faith of Jesus Christ. Since the power exists to over power such evil, it must be appropriated by each and every believer and utilized to its fullest to wage warfare against the evil forces that come against the Christian way of life.

Eureka, I have found (it)!

Eureka is a word used to express triumph upon finding or discovering something of value. My paternal grandmother was a saint, at least in my book. She loved God, her husband, her children, and practiced her faith on a daily basis. Since marriage and family were an integral part of her Christian life, the loss of her wedding ring while gardening was a severe blow. There was no money to buy another ring: in fact, she wanted the one used in her wedding ceremony. Nothing would truly satisfy her except the original gold band.

Years of hoping, praying and occasionally fretting about her lost wedding band passed until one day her son William was digging in the garden and found a little piece of gold. Rushing to his mother with his marvelous find, the dirt was removed and the gold was washed clean. A "whoop and a holler" reverberated from the kitchen that could be heard on the next three farms. She did not use the word "eureka", but she had the sense of triumph at finding something of great value. Something she held dear, a vital part of who she was, and a gift that could not be replaced with a substitute, had been found. Grandmother felt whole again; she had her original wedding band. Could it not be the same with us? Re-discovering the first love that came with conversion and the first generational resistance to all things evil, victorious warfare could be waged against evil. Joy and victory could return to the soul and mind of all who follow Christ.

Have we lost the joy of first love? Are we willing to settle for substitutes for valued spiritual things? Are we satisfied with "playing church" without the power to change the world around us? What needs to be restored? Are we patient and persistent in prayer and work...searching until those precious things are restored? "Weeping may endure for the night, but joy comes in the morning!" Until then, work and prayer is the proper response. Talking about the issues does not change things. Prayer changes people and people change things. Joy in the camp will not be restored until the fight for those valued areas of moral and spiritual life is adequately waged against the enemy.

The Slumbering Force of Hope

The twilight of spiritual truth may be eclipsed by the darkness of the times, but beneath the despair of the people is the slumbering force of indestructible hope. This hope is in the Resurrected Christ and it brings with it the power of a sacred responsibility. This incorruptible hope will guide believers to develop a strategy to behave what they believe!

Nonetheless, the battle lines have been drawn and the forces of evil are in rank and ready to destroy the remaining influence of organized religion in society. This is normally done by the weakening of spiritual leadership and the disgrace and disqualification of individuals of prominence. Believers must develop a strategic attack plan to protect what is sacred and to behave what they believe. It is time to resist. It is time to re-consecrate the Christian leadership for true and undefiled ministry. It is time to wage war against the forces that would destroy the useful function of Christianity in society and its ongoing influence. It is time to behave what we believe.

Reading the Bible and Behaving it!

Visiting Hong Kong some years back a story was shared about a young convert who wrote his mother on the Mainland that he was reading the bible and behaving it. Putting the story in the Preface of a book, the typist changed the words to read: "Reading the Bible and Believing it." Sending the copy back for correction, she said "I have never heard of behaving the Bible; I was taught to believe it." Sadly, this is too often true of too many. It is time for all good Christians to read and behave the words of the Good Book.

The Human Condition

Mankind has been in trouble since the Serpent

beguiled Eve and Adam was tempted and disobeyed God. From the description of Job's trouble in the Old Testament, to the front page news stories and 24/7 television programming, it is clear that modern life is not a bed of roses. Even when a person accepts the saving grace of Christ and becomes a new creation, that individual remains a part of the human race. One may have the assurance of salvation and still not clearly understand the forces of evil that plot against faith and good practices. It is the liability of this human condition, that some have called the "original sin equation" and this sin equation accounts for most of the difficulties in families and communities. It is the work of the human element that complicates the troubled situations in the institutions that would seek to change the world.

In addition to the original condition of the unconverted, and the untaught nature of some believers, there is the presence of evil in the world. Satan is a Hebrew word, signifying an adversary, or enemy -- an accuser. Most commonly Satan is taken for the Devil, or chief of the evil spirits. Satan is also behind those adversaries of Christianity who seemed filled with a malignant spirit in their persecution of believers.

It is time to wage spiritual warfare against Satan and the forces of evil that work in the world. We can no longer attempt to build Christian institutions through programs and personality; prayer is required. The passive assent to truth and righteousness is not sufficient. There must be a clear and formal declaration of war against evil to adequately mobilize the troops for the struggle between good and evil. We must behave what we believe.

An Organized Resistance

It is time for real and personal commitment to an organized resistance against Satan's influence in the world. Evil has infiltrated the sacred ranks of the clergy, discord has taken refuge in the choir, lethargic laymen fill the pews, drowsy deacons carelessly serve, and dull preachers discourage those who seek grace and forgiveness. There are few champions to challenge the young to join the battle. Where are the modern heroes of the faith? There are few heroes for the young to use as role models. Public personalities have "public" moral failure, and when Satan presents himself, as a wolf in sheep's clothing, some believers are unable to discern the difference.

Careless behavior and a carnal lifestyle are accepted as normal. The thought of living in contrast to the evil society, as a witness for Christ, is repugnant to many who claim membership in Christian organizations. The idea of holiness has been discarded on the ash heap of clergy sins. The concept of sacred things engrained in the culture by the founding fathers is cast aside for political correctness.

Children are taught in a secular system where science is more powerful than scripture, where evolution has replaced creation, where even Intelligent Design is frowned upon because it hints at a divine creator. In the eyes of many, man is little more than an advanced animal. No wonder some brutish and bestial behavior is justified and sinful behavior is downplayed and explained in terms of sickness or upbringing. Somehow believers must stand in the gap and pray and organize resistance against the evil in the world.

Satan, as a Roaring Lion

In the days of Job, the people of God came "to present themselves before the Lord", and Satan came also and presented himself as an Angel of Light. When God asked Satan where he had been, Satan's answer was simply, "From going to and fro in the earth, and from walking up and down in it." Following this encounter came Job's great test. (Job 1:6-8) Satan is still roaming the earth seeking to destroy individuals and hinder the Cause of Christ. Yes, Satan still attends the places of worship. He may also be found in the choir and on the deacon's bench. How else could one explain the turmoil that exists within many congregations, if it were not instigated by Satan? And increased by carnal members who seek personal advantage rather than advancing the Kingdom.

Evil is an active force around the world seeking to destroy the good. (1 Peter 5:8-11) Satan, as a roaring lion, walks about, seeking whom he may devour. Believers are told to resist steadfast in the faith and God will bring the victory. We may not clearly understand how, but Christians must launch a strategic offensive against the forces of evil that would destroy all that is good in the world.

> Bow down before the strong hand of God, that in His good time He may lift you up. Throw back on Him the burden of your anxiety; because He cares for you. Have a thoughtful demeanor, be on guard, because your enemy the devil, prowls about as an angry lion, seeking someone to greedily consume. Be strong in faith and stand up to the devil, knowing that you share the same suffering with your brothers all over the world. And the God of all grace who has called us to enjoy His eternal glory in Christ Jesus, after you suffer a little He will restore, strengthen, and establish you as a resident

of heaven. 11. To Him be glory and power through endless ages, Amen. (1 Peter 5:6-11 EDNT)

Strength in Numbers

There is strength in numbers, safety in community, and victory in teamwork. To utilize the strength gained from numbers, secure the safety provided by community, and gain the victory through teamwork, more must be known about strongholds and the spiritual darkness that plagues the earth. We need truth and enlightenment from the Holy Spirit as we seek to determine possible conditions that create spiritual darkness and the circumstance that permits such wickedness to linger. No individual alone can adequately fight Satan, the evil effects of sin in the world. There must be a family, a community, a congregation, a band of believers, a gathering of friends, a Nation that protects and provides opportunity to hear and receive the Gospel.

Together, believers can structure a crusade of resistance. With the assistance of others, individuals can adequately resist the forces of evil and maintain a Christian lifestyle. We must bear one another's burdens. There is strength in unity. The more we understand about the spiritual battlefield, the better the organized resistance will be.

Reasons for Lingering Darkness

What areas of lingering spiritual darkness are present? What factors are present that could establish demonic strongholds? What could be the antecedent cause for the present problems in communities and churches? Why has it been so difficult through the years to establish a growing spiritual congregation in some areas? What causes some local congregations to self-destruct when they seem to have such potential? Why have so many clergy and church staff lapsed into immorality? What has happened to the keepers of the Gates?

Secular Humanism

The dominance of education by secular humanism is a growing factor in satanic opposition to the Biblical record and religious traditions. Education goes to the heart of the family and when conflicting worldviews are taught, the young are confused and some are deceived. Peer pressure in school can cause children from Christian families to go along with the textbooks written by individuals who do not accept Intelligent Design, Creation or the Bible record of history. A pluralistic culture and the conflict of traditional religion with the New Age Movement, secular humanism, and the current impact of materialism including the class struggle between the poor and the rich can create fertile ground for evil to work.

Atheism, Agnosticism, and Injustice

The knowledge that atheist and agnostics function freely in education, government, and public life creates doubt as to the validity of the Christian message. The lack of equal justice under the law for certain crimes and the disproportional punishment for others creates mistrust. The concept of equality under the law is broken down and the idea of inalienable rights from God is challenged. When some or all of these things exist in a community, it may well be a stronghold of evil. When any of these conflicts exist in a community it will cause the spiritual darkness to linger, deepen and eventually open the way for a satanic stronghold.

Through the power of the Holy Spirit, the authority of the Word of God, and prayer and fasting, these and other evil influences could be over come. What is needed is for a few committed believers to provide a Joshua and Caleb response to the obvious giants in the land. This type of minority report (we are able to take the land) could secure a firm commitment from local congregations, and create a body of Christians determined to take back what the enemy has occupied and to re-consecrate the holy places: the family altar, the family pew, and the family table where parents can adequately guide a growing family in faith and conduct.

Where is the man who will say with Caleb, "Give me this mountain" (referring to the strongholds of the giants)? Joshua and Caleb had developed an understanding of the enemy and had a strategy to take back the Promised Land from the giants. We can open the door to true enlightenment and teach the truth. We can speak and act with the boldness of the Spirit, but not alone. This work requires basic teamwork, a spiritual togetherness, continued intercessory prayer, and God-given boldness to enable and encourage participation in spiritual warfare. Where are those willing to stand together and conquer the strongholds of evil that plague family and community life?

Overcome Evil with Good

> 9. Let love be without hypocrisy. Hate what is wrong. Cleave to the good. 10. Have tender affection for the believers; go before one another as an honorable guide; 11. do not delay your enthusiasm; be on fire in the spirit; serving the Lord as a slave; 12. rejoice in hope; remain steadfast in time of trouble; be persistent in the habit of prayer; 13. contribute your share with reference to the needs of the saints; give attention to hospitality. 14. Bless all who persecute you: bless and curse not. 15. Share the happiness of those who rejoice, and share the sorrow of those who are sad. 16. Maintain harmony with one another. Set your mind on high things, but accept

humble ways. Do not think too highly of yourself. 17. Never pay back injury for injury. Aim to do what is honorable in the sight of all men. 18. As much as you can, live peaceable with all men. 19. Never avenge yourselves dearly beloved, but leave room for Gods anger: for it is written, Vengeance is mine; I will repay, said the Lord. 20. There is another test, if your enemy hunger, feed him; if he thirst, give him drink: for in so doing you will make him feel a burning sense of shame. 21. Never permit evil to conquer you, but get the better of evil by doing good. (Romans 12:9-21 EDNT)

CHAPTER THREE

A Strategy Against Strongholds

*Like a mighty army,
Moves the Church of God
Brothers, we are treading
Where the saints have trod.
We are not divided, all one body we
One in hope and doctrine, One in charity.*

- Sabine Baring-Gould -

Walls Cannot Protect

No investment of money, men, and material is sufficient to protect individuals or institutions from outside forces when the priest of the family or the keeper of the gates of society can be distracted or disarmed. There must be a strategy to protect those principles and values that are sacred in a moral society. Walls cannot protect a society from itself. When Robert C. Byrd was the Junior Senator from West Virginia, he spoke at a meeting of the Gideons. He had committed to memory many details about the Great Wall of China. The wall was 4,160 miles across Northern China. It was the only man made structure that was visible from the moon with the naked eye. Wall construction started as far back as Chinese recorded history. Prisoners of war, convicts, soldiers, civilians and farmers provided the labor. Millions died for this cause, and many Chinese stories speak of parted lovers and men dying of starvation and disease. Materials used for the wall, were whatever could be found near by; clay, stone, willow branches, reeds and sand. Thousands of bodies have been discovered buried in the foundations of the wall, or used to make up its thickness.

The people listened closely as he told of the years it took to build the wall and the cost of material and lives. Particularly, how workers who died on the job were entombed in the wall. The wall was built to keep China's enemies from attacking or conquering sections of the country. History suggests that the wall worked well when the country was strong. Only when a dynasty had weakened from within, were invaders from the north able to advance and conquer. In the many years since the wall was completed, not a single invader has breached the wall. They did not have to scale the wall or break it down; they simply bribed the keepers of the gates. In reality, no wall of protection is stronger than the individuals and the institutions that guard the gates. Where are the strong men that should be standing watch? Who will give the signal that the enemy is near? Who will rally the spiritual troops for this conflict? Where have all the warriors gone?

A Summons to Spiritual Combat

The opposite of what is true in the local congregation is a fact in the world of evil. God gives spiritual gifts to individuals, and places these gifted individuals in institutions and organizations for edification and ministry. Jesus told Andrew and Peter that he would make them "fishers of men"(Matthew 4:19). The word used to illustrate catching fish was defined as "catching alive." The same word is used only one other time in the New Testament in 2 Timothy 2:26 Paul spoke of men who had been caught in the snare to do the devil's will. Thus, some are caught alive to do the devil's work. The strongholds of spiritual darkness are established and hinder the propagation of the Gospel. Believers are summoned to spiritual combat daily. We must engage the enemy.

Perpetual Wickedness

Perpetual wickedness and pervasive evil are established where spiritual darkness lingers. These are areas where the spiritual domain is inhabited by non-Christians and controlled by individuals who are controlled by demonic entities. The particular localities where such controlled humans reside will exhibit the influence of demonic entities. This creates evil cross currents in the society and serious moral and spiritual conflict among the people. It requires spiritual power to resist such forces on a community. Many doubt that such occasions exist, but evidence points to the truth of the matter.

A Counterfeit World View

Satan seeks to counterfeit the fellowship and brotherhood of the Christian movement through a network of strongholds. The compelling interchange of human philosophy, evil commotions, negative nostalgia, coded numerology, fables, legends and myths, have been used to counterfeit a world view contrary to the Biblical record and establish strongholds that permit the proliferation of evil. These things must be continually resisted.

A Diverse and Tempestuous Past

Early Christianity had to fight against flawed and entrenched religious beliefs which had existed for centuries. Most of the beliefs degenerated into feeble superstitions and meaningless rituals, but some flourished in areas of spiritual darkness and became evil strongholds. The religious beliefs of a pagan society give man no hope and produce a lingering spiritual darkness that has covered much of the populated world. This has left many destitute of moral and spiritual purpose.

Much of the known world have a tempestuous past. The spiritual darkness is evident on many mission fields. In one country a small effort wins many. Yet, in another country great effort has little results. Even within the same mission field there are places and people more receptive to the gospel. Surely, what is true on the mission fields of the world is true in the cities and towns around the world. This is not recognized by many spiritual leaders and this complicates the problem and produces unwarned and unprepared people who are taken captive by evil forces to do the devil's bidding.

Strongholds are Strengthened

The pluralism of culture and various religious traditions contributes to the forces of evil at work in some institutions and in the personal practices of some individuals who claim to be Christian. Evil strongholds are strengthened and reaffirmed when succeeding generations unknowingly practice certain rituals and traditions. Demonic strongholds are strengthened by several factors: the substance of the original sinful alliance in a particular place, the character of the evil spirits involved in the alliance, and the duration the evil alliance goes unchallenged by concerted spiritual opposition. Why is this so? In the past when evil was weak in a given community, people tolerated the evil and it grew. Their eyes became accustomed to the darkness. It is just as if someone neglected to place available medicine on an infection. It grows worse and worse until it requires drastic action.

Division, Neglect, and Sin

Organized religion has been weakened by division, neglect, and sin and has not made a concerted effort to withstand the onslaughts of Satan on the modern world. First, there was the conflict between Judaism and Christianity during the founding period. Then, it was the Protestant-Catholic conflict during the Middle Ages. And, now, the pluralistic society has opened the door for other world religions to be presented as equal to Christianity. In fact some Eastern religions are given freedoms that are denied the traditional Christian movement. This is done in the name of tolerance and political correctness. This further entrenches practices and traditions that work against the Christian faith and weaken the will to resist the forces of evil encroachment.

The pluralistic culture with multiple national origins has precipitated the division of Protestantism into over three-hundred denominations with as many as 21,000 different doctrinal positions on Scriptural interpretation. This has complicated any national call for moral renewal. There is no agreement on the concept of morality or personal ethics. The technological, secular, and impersonal society of today seeks a moral code radically different from the one declared throughout Scripture or the code taught from the formation of the American States. In fact, some of the original states had stronger Christian statements in their State Constitutions than the Federal Constitution we treasure so dearly. The small compromises to obtain unity opened the door for the wedge of political correctness at the expense of many traditional values. One may ask, "Is there any hope for change for the better in society?" The answer is little if any hope outside of divine intervention or total cooperation and unity among believers.

The Only Hope

The only hope is for individual believers to join together, forgetting their sectarian differences, and formulate a strategy to wage war against evil and stand in the gap and pray. The moral high ground can be reclaimed if the battle is waged on all fronts. It can never happen with one political party, or one denomination, or even one religion making the battle. It will take total agreement among all men of good will. Without the moral high ground, the battle against evil strongholds will fail. This can only be done through claiming certain common moral ground and fortifying the mind and heart with a common denominator agenda that relates to the welfare of the individual, the strengthening of the family, the restoration of pure religion, with the full participation of believers in the political process. A personal pledge to ethical and moral living by each individual would enhance this effort. It has to start someplace. Why not with your community, your congregation, your family? In this way, the fight against Satan, strengthened through prayer and fasting, will win. It can be done. It must be done and you and your family can be part of the solution, but we must stand in the gap and pray and resist.

Satan and his cohorts cannot stand before a blood washed band of believers determined to win the battle against evil. The Word is clear: "Submit yourselves therefore to God. Resist the devil, and he will flee from you." (James 4:6) The concept here of "submit" suggests the urgent lining up under the authority of God as a force to "resist" or stand against the devil and with God's assistance the devil will run from the battlefield. Satan and his cohorts know they were defeated at Mount Calvary and do not wish to tangle with the mighty army of Christ. Who will join this band of believers? Who will take up the

Sword of the Spirit and stand against the onslaught of evil? (James 4:6,8)

> 7. Be God's true subjects; stand firm against the devil, and he will vanish from you. 8. Bow down before God, and He will be near your hand. You who have erred and missed the mark must cleanse your hands, and you who have wavered or are two-spirited must free your thoughts and feelings from guilt. 9. Bow yourself down with sorrow and let weeping turn your delight to sadness. 10. Bring yourself low before God and He will exalt you. (James 4:7-10 EDNT)

A Sense of Unity among Believers

What can Christians do to protect themselves and their institutions from the evil forces that press upon them daily? There must be both a sense of unity among believers and a spiritual commitment by individual believers to permit the Spirit to actively work on their behalf. This requires a lifestyle that speaks of commitment, faith, hope, and charity. Without both sharing the message of faith and supporting the basic needs of the poor, there can be no moral victory.

The storing of wealth for a personal rainy day when the flood has already overtaken the less fortunate is both non-Christian and does not measure up to the dream of equality and justice for all. To stand in the gap and pray, we must go beyond sexual purity, marriage fidelity, and basic honesty. There must be a commitment to public justice, equal opportunity, the sharing of wealth, and support of the needy. Armed with both hope and charity of heart, intercessory prayer can bring a united ministry, together the collective body of believers can withstand the offensive of Satan and bring social justice to the world. The wise man Solomon declared

> 9. Two are better than one; because they have a good reward for their labor. 10. For if they fall, the one will lift up his fellow:

but woe, to him that is alone when he falleth; for he hath not another to help him up." (Ecclesiastes 4:9.10)

Believers must work together and walk together with confidence that, together, they can win the victory over evil.

The Best Defense

To be forewarned is to be forearmed. On a personal level, the best defense is to acknowledge that satanic powers exist and are at work in the world. Also, to be aware of the devices that Satan uses to defeat individual believers and to bring disharmony and disunity within the gathered church. We must not be ignorant of Satan's strategies or the devices used by his cohorts. We must put on the whole armor of God in order to withstand the evil darts of the devil. We must unite and support one another in prayer and a clear affirmation of faith.

> 10. Finally, my brothers, be strengthened in the Lord, and in the power of His unlimited resource. 11. Wear the complete armor of God, so you can stand against the strategy and assault of the adversary. 12. For our wrestling is not against a physical enemy, but against evil princes of darkness who rule this world, against hosts of spiritual wickedness in heavenly warfare. 13. Wherefore wear the complete armor of God that you may be able to withstand evil attacks when they come, and be found still standing. 14. Stand your ground, being protected by Truth, and having integrity for a breastplate; 15. and the gospel of peace preparing your feet for battle, 16. above all, take the shield of faith to extinguish all the fiery darts of the wicked. 17. And take the helmet, which is salvation, and the sword of the Spirit, which is the word of God: 18. praying on every occasion through petition in the Spirit, and be vigilant with unwearied perseverance and supplication for all saints; (Ephesians 6:10-18 EDNT)

Many Unanswered Questions

There are many unanswered questions. Why does spiritual darkness linger? How do Christians arrive at a complete understanding of the spiritual battlefield? How does ones worldview influence their awareness of the supernatural and the demonic? How does the present action of individuals and the gathered church cause spiritual darkness to linger?

Spiritual darkness lingers because Christians do not obey God and resist Satan. Christian institutions must not depend on naturalistic explanations derived from the social sciences to explain why spiritual darkness remains in certain places. The evidence is clear concerning an objective Devil in the Biblical record and the affirmations regarding the existence of demonic spiritual beings is consistent with the personal experience of many. James clearly spoke to the issue of obedience and acknowledged the need for praising God and a clear injunction to resist Satan. James declared that man's own desires entice him to evil and this strengthens the spiritual darkness in the world. (James 4:7-10)

This is not a Game

Just as any commander, when Satan sees an increase in Christian effectiveness in a particular area, he will send his cohorts to confuse and corrupt the process. As missions and evangelism increase in given areas, one can expect demonic entrenchment and demonic desperation correspondingly to the increase in soul-winning. As institutions become effective in redirecting energies toward changing the world, evil forces will be weakened. .Thus, all Christian institutions involved in missionary outreach and evangelism need to take measures to ensure their protection while they seek to uproot the strongholds of evil that currently hinder their progress.

This is not a game; it is warfare. We must be equipped with the whole armor of God to withstand the evil and achieve significant advance of the Gospel message.

A Challenge to Pray

This volume will not answer all these questions, but the Good Book is full of helpful suggestions. It is hopeful that this effort will challenge individual believers to get into the Word, to resist Satan and to unite with one another to weaken the evil strongholds on families, institutions, the pluralistic culture, and the political system. The human bondage to evil forces is rooted in human rebellion against God (Romans 1:18-32) and evil desires (James 1:14). The human mind is a force utilized by evil entities to further the process of demonic activity. Believers must guard well what goes in totheir mind.

This challenge must come though prayer and use of the Word of God as a force of Truth against the evil forces. How may believers and the gathered church be protected from the influence of past evil alliances and present demonic activity? Christians must take initiatives that target evil strongholds. (2 Corinthians 4:4)

> 1. Therefore seeing we have this commission, as received by the mercy of God, we do not get discouraged; 2. but have renounced disgraceful and underhanded ways, we do not practice trickery or adulterate the word of God; only by openly declaring the truth we recommend ourselves to the honest judgment of man in the sight of God. 3. But if our gospel is veiled, it is veiled to the lost: 4. whose unbelieving minds are blinded by the god of this world, lest the image of God and the glorious light of the gospel of Christ should shine unto them. (2 Corinthians 4:1-4 EDNT)

Any collective efforts to break down strongholds should be rooted in scripture as a methodology to provide opportunity for individuals to hear and respond to the

A STRATEGY AGAINST STRONGHOLDS

Christian message. The Word and togetherness in prayer are the basic weapons.

> 2. Persevere in prayer and remain alert and thankful; 3. include us in your prayers, that God would give us an open door for the word, to speak of the sacred secrets of Christ, for which I am in prison: 4. that I may explain the secrets. 5. Behave with wisdom toward non-Christians, buying up every opportunity. 6. Always make your speech pleasing and tasteful, that you may know how to give a proper answer to every question. (Colossians 4:22-6 EDNT)

This may be only a temporary lifting of spiritual blindness that allows individuals to accept Christ. The forces of evil remain to attack their decision and their future lifestyle. The gathered believers must provide a strategy to withstand continuing demonic attacks. There should be a sense of institutional repentance and release from past sins, together with spiritual counter offensives against evil and continued efforts at spiritual and moral renewal.

> Human beings we may be, but we do not fight our battles in human strength: the weapons we use to fight are not human, but mighty through God to demolish strongholds; (2 Corinthians 10:3, 4 EDNT)

> Persevere in prayer and remain alert and thankful; include us in your prayers, that God would give us an open door for the word, to speak of the sacred secrets of Christ, for which I am in prison: 4. that I may explain the secrets. Behave with wisdom toward non-Christians, buying up every opportunity. Always make your speech pleasing and tasteful, that you may know how to give a proper answer to every question. (Colossians 4:2-6 EDNT)

Understand the Battlefield

Present day believers must understand the material world in which the spiritual battles are being waged. The material world, the unregenerate population, the corrupt world system, and the carnality of professing Christians contribute to the weakness of the gathered church to fight the good fight of faith and finish the course with honor and victory. Modern believers should be encouraged to emulate Joshua and Caleb (Numbers 13) who claimed the territory of the giants as their own and declared their faith in Divine enabling to defeat all opposition to possession of the promised land. Following the example of Joshua and Caleb, we can stand in the gap and pray and get on with the business of the Great Commission.

A Strategic Plan

A strategic plan for the pulling down of strongholds to bring spiritual light into the lingering darkness may be taken from the forty day mission to spy out the land (Numbers 13). This mission required one leader from each group and was to be accomplished in secret. The leaders were given specific instructions as to what their specific objectives were to include. An examination of the mission objectives of the men sent to secretly observe the strength of the enemy and the possible resources for building would be a good place to start the planning process. Their strategic objectives were:

1. Measure the strength of the enemy.
2. Survey the nature of the land.
3. Observe the kind of people who live there.
4. Appraise the cities level of development.
5. Evaluate the productivity of the land.
6. Determine the available material for building.
7. Maintain fearless resistance and fortitude.
8. Examine the fruit and bring back evidence.

A Minority Report

After a negative report of the mission, Joshua and Caleb gave a minority report that was positive. Caleb stilled the people before Moses and said, "Let us go up at once, and possess it; for we are well able to overcome it." The majority will always have an evil report, but a few committed believers can and will overcome evil and break down the demonic strongholds. Prayer and spiritual weapons based on a firm understanding of scripture are God's instruments against evil strongholds. As God prompts, we must act. We must stand in the gap and pray and give the next generation a chance to study in a moral environment under Christian teachers in committed institutions.

Prayer Required

Whom shall we send and who will go for us? Who is willing to make the commitment? One must be prepared to deal with evil forces. Certain evil strongholds and certain spirits require special preparation. When Jesus healed a boy possessed with a demon, his disciples asked:

> And when He had entered the house, His disciples asked privately, Why were we unable to cast out the spirit? And Jesus answered, *This kind can come out by nothing except prayer.* (Mark 9:28, 29 EDNT)

> *v29 Although fasting is an important teaching, the words "and fasting" here were not adequately supported by the original texts.

Kindred Minds Joined in Heart

Are you willing to make the commitment and join forces with others with kindred minds? Will you be joined in heart with those who want to resist Satan? To do so you must be prepared to fight the good fight and pursue the enemy into his own territory. You must go forth together in mind and heart with concern for yourself and those with whom you serve. Remember, Paul's challenge to Timothy:

> 11. These things learn and teach with authority. 12. Permit no man to look down on your youthfulness; show yourself a pattern of believers in speech, in behavior, in love, in faith, in sexual purity. 13. Until I come, grace the public reading of scripture with your presence and speak and teach encouraging words. 14. Do not neglect the spiritual endowment you possess, which was given you by means of prophecy, with the laying on of the hands of preaching elders. 15. Give attention to these things; give yourself wholly to them; that your progress may appear to all. 16. Take heed to yourself and continue in the teaching; for in doing this you will both save yourself and the ones hearing you. 16. If any believing woman have widows, let her assist them, leaving the church to support the widows who are destitute. (1 Timothy 4:11-16 EDNT)

CHAPTER FOUR

Kindred Minds Joined In Heart

> Our fathers, chained in prisons dark,
> Were still in heart and conscience free:
> How sweet would be their children's fate,
> If they like them could die for thee!
> Faith of our fathers, holy faith!
> We will be true to thee till death!
>
> - Frederick W. Faber -

An Unnamed Woman Who Understood her Identity

It is amazing how knowing one's identity and the boldness to witness could change a murdering rapist into a studious believer. A letter came from the Texas State Prison requesting books from the library. It was from Steve Moran on Death Row. Since the graduate school did not loan books, volumes were sent from my personal library. A friend in North Carolina also sent Bible study books. Later my son, Barton, interviewed Steve and wrote a book about his conversion. I learned that Steve had killed several women in Texas and was under 13 death sentences. Notwithstanding his criminal past, Steve had experienced a genuine conversion and knew his "identity". He was hungry to learn all he could about the Christian faith. His conversion is a great untold story!

Another letter came from Steve. The date had been set for his execution and he shared, "I am guilty and will not appeal." He returned the books, together with a list of what he had read since being on Death Row. It was impressive. He assured me that he had read all the books and was ready for his final exam. He asked to keep one book, a modern version of *Pilgrim's Progress*. It was later returned after his execution. At the close of the letter, Steve thanked me for teaching him a reading and study system and supplying study books. Steve expressed good thoughts for the work of the school and closed by saying, "In a few days I will meet God. I will not die as other men. I have been saved. I will give my life for crimes committed, but my soul is safe." The letter ended with a profound statement, "When I see God, I will tell him about you." Steve knew his identity as a believer.

Steve Moran died by lethal injection. I have thought often about one woman's witness that led to Steve Moran's conversion, Steve's awareness that he would soon see God and speak to Him face to face about me, spoke clearly about his readiness to die. Of course, God already knew the facts, but somehow it gave a different twist to the whole process to see how a young man, converted after a life of crime and condemned to die, would see a simple act of Christian charity. It gave me confidence that small acts of kindness are remembered and surely recorded in the Master Record Book.

Due to legal conflicts with the principals, the book (*Hostage from Heaven*) about the life and conversion of Steve Moran was never published. It is a story of rape, murder, great conflict, and the courage of one unnamed woman who understood her identity as a Christian and avoided rape by witnessing of God's saving Grace. Steve's conversion was a significant victory in the battle against evil and should be told. It is documented evidence that one believer, with spiritual boldness, can resist evil and win. It also speaks about the other 113 women murdered by Steve during his life of crime. Who failed to teach them that through conversion they could gain power to resist the devil and his forces? Anyone of the victims was a person and, with the help of God, could have stopped Steve just as the unnamed believer did. Who failed those victims?

Identity is in the Things one Values

My father died when I was four. As a child, my family constantly told me about my father. How brave he was in going to get the cow up a dark hallow and whistling all the way. He was good with a rifle. He enjoyed cars. He always wanted to be dressed up, neat and clean. He was a young Deacon with zeal for helping other young men find their path in life. He was a good husband; a good father, and a man with a zeal for lost souls.

Daddy had rheumatic fever as a child and was told that he would not live to see manhood. He married and fathered three children. His widow survived him by 60 years. The fever affected his heart; he was only 30 when he died. His identity is tied up in the things he valued. I have three things that were his: a pair of gold rimmed glasses, a whet stone for which he carved a wooden box with his name on it, and a walking stick with his initials carved for all to see. These items are precious to me and conjure up various images and ideas about my father. Most of all I identify with him through these objects and they tell me things he would want me to know.

The glasses, he wore everyday, say look daily at life; it is precious. Daddy had a philosophy which he called, G.O.A.L., "Get Out And Live." See the flowers and don't let physical limitations stop you. He knew his life would be short, but it was filled with work, worship, play, fishing, hunting, wife, children, brothers, sisters, and friends. During his short life he established an identity.

The wooden box and whet stone were made during a 1924 trip to Hot Springs, Arkansas to take hot baths and recover his strength. He used it regularly to keep his pocket knife sharp. The box and the whet stone clearly points out that one's tools must be ready. It declares that honest work is good for the soul and the box with the date and his name carved on it speaks to anyone and says, "I was here. I was real. Don't forget me." In fact, his brothers showed me rocks and trees on which he carved his initials a special way. He made just one deep stroke into the bark of a tree with his knife and let the growth of the tree over time reveal his initials. On the rocks, he always went to the underneath side or the overhang protected from the weather. He was proud of his identity. He wanted to be remembered. Those who carved out the letters so one could see them immediately had their initials soon disfigured by tree growth, but the growth over time just make daddy's initials more prominent. "HBG was here; don't forget me!"

The walking stick was used in a forced effort to remain active and live up to his motto, "Get Out And Live." He was active and worked the last day of his life, then took a car load of young men to a revival meeting. He returned after the family was asleep. With the baby in bed with mother, daddy hung his clothes on a chair, slipped into the foot of the bed in an effort not to disturb, and died in his sleep. The walking stick is useful. It assists and comforts me in times of need. After an operation and prior to and following knee surgery, daddy's walking stick was used. With each step I could feel his hand escorting me forward. I could almost hear a soft voice saying, "Keep pushing, son, don't let it get you down." An uncle said if you take that black paint off you will find Barton's initials somewhere. I did and there they were -- "HBG."

I had two other personal mementos; his pocket knife and his favorite 12 gage shotgun. I lost the knife as a child and the gun was stolen on a cold Christmas Eve.

Both losses were painful. The gun had a mighty kick. I have a picture of the last turkey daddy shot with the gun. Somewhere daddy's bird gun is hanging over a mantle, but they don't know the stories that go with the gun nor do they know the man who owned and used the gun. (Down inside are the initials HBG, someday I may find it).

The knife and the gun are gone, one through my childish carelessness, the other because of a thief. Even these lost items remind me to be careful with things that are dear and valuable. Thoughts of the stolen gun remind me that there are still people in the world who are "takers" and that everyone must be watchful and protective of both property and heritage. The memories and the life daddy lived are real. He knew who he was and wanted to identify with the things he valued. He took an active role in politics and worked to get good, honest, and decent people elected. He was a good soldier in the Lord's Army. Sometimes the good die young. Others must pick up the torch and the sword and move forward into battle.

A Soldier's Identity

The congregation by its essential character and definition should be a group of kindred minds joined in heart and concerned about the community in which they live. Since spiritual leaders know this characterization of the congregation to be accurate, why is there so little action in the battle? Why is it so difficult to get spiritual soldiers to identify with the cause and stand up to protect the community from attacks of evil? In order to field Christian soldiers in sufficient numbers to make a significant difference in the battle for morality, the gathered believers should take a fresh look at the pristine form and function of the congregation.

> 3. Join the ranks of those who share hardships as a soldier of Jesus Christ. 4. No active warrior entangles himself with ordinary affairs; so he may please the one who enlisted him as a soldier. 5. And also if anyone wrestles, he is not crowned unless he wrestles lawfully. (2 Timothy 2:3-5 EDNT)

Struggle for Identity

Peter saw the early gathering of believers as it struggled for identity. He witnessed a company of believers committed to a cause and separated from the world as a redeemed community serving the needs of one another.

> 9. But you are a chosen race, a royal priesthood, a dedicated nation, and a people God means to have for Himself, that you might show forth His praises who called you out of darkness into His amazing light. 10. There was a time when you were not a people, now you are God's people because you obtained mercy. (1 Peter 2: 9, 10 EDNT)

Concept of the City-State

The concept of the city-state in history was a model for the way the congregation understood itself and others. The city was walled for protection of those who lived within the gates, known as "citizens" People who lived beyond the walls, on the heath (pasture land with low shrubs), were called "heathen," a loose rendering to the Latin for pagan. Others who lived still farther beyond the heath in the woods or forest were known as "savages" or tree dwellers. Travelers who passed the gates of the city were called "foreigners" or "strangers" and were mistrusted. Those who mounted armed assault against the city or simply harassed the citizens were known as "the enemy."

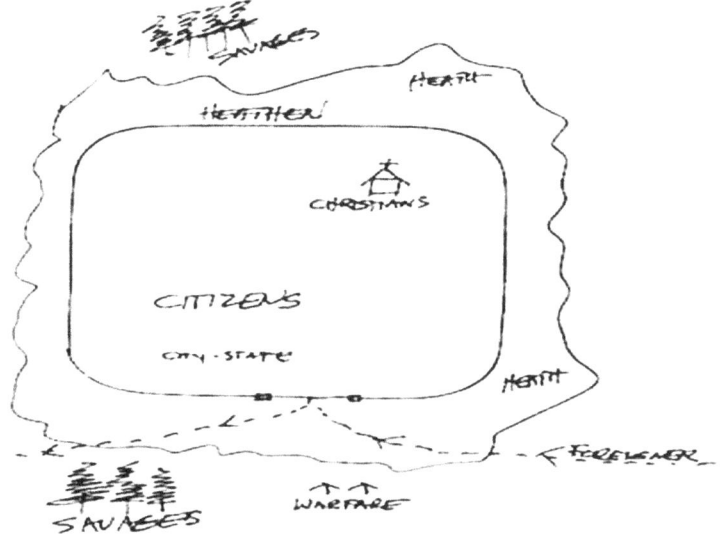

When the strong men of the city went outside the protected sanctuary of the walls to drive off an enemy, they engaged in "warfare." One can easily see the connection between the city-state concept and the way the congregation understands their life and mission? Casual observers of a local church can see a few similarities.

The organized church sends missionaries to the heathen and the savages. Foreigners are stilled looked upon as being different, meaning "unlike us;" therefore, not as good as we are. Such attitudes breed false pride, bigotry, intolerance, discrimination, prejudice, and favoritism. Of course, this complicates any effort to unify the congregation for the spiritual battles that must be fought to guard the faith and stand in the gap and pray.

The people who lived within the gates were called "citizens" and were under the protection of the keepers of the gates and the select assembly. If the keepers of the gates signaled all to assemble inside the city walls, the warriors then went to the walls to guard the people or resist the attacker.

The New Testament was a book of cities. Congregations were established in the cities where the people lived and worked. If one notes the mission and ministry of Paul he was primarily on a journey from Jerusalem the religious center to Rome the political center of the world of his day. Paul never bothered with small towns or rural communities. His mission was to take the message to the citizens of the cities and transform these citizens into Christians. Constantly we see Paul on his way to Rome. Since the Christian congregations were established in the cities, it is easy to see how the early believers translated the idea of good citizens into the concept of Christians.

A View of a City-State

When the early revival came to Antioch and Barnabas needed assistance in disciplining the new converts, he invited Paul to come to the city and assist with the teaching. The scripture is clear:

> 25. Then Barnabas went to Tarsus in search of Saul: 26. and when he found Saul brought him to Antioch. And for one whole year they assembled with the church and taught many people. And the disciples first began to transact their affairs as Christians in Antioch.* 27. At this time prophets from Jerusalem came to Antioch. 28. And one of them came forward named Agabus and predicted by the Spirit that a famine was to visit the whole world: and it did happen in the time of Claudius. 29. Then every disciple according to his ability determined to send relief to the brethren in Judaea: 30. this they did and sent it to the elders by Barnabas and Saul.

*v26 At first it was a life-style recognized by others, then it became a mark of identification as a follower of Christ.

And the disciples were called Christians first in Antioch." (Acts 11:26) The converted "citizens" after a one year disciple training program became known as "Christians." The historical church eagerly added the rest of the city-state language to their mission. The added vocabulary included such words as heathen, savage, foreigner, enemy, and warfare. What happened to the special "citizen's council," *the called out ones* who functioned to equip and protect the church? The church has both a spiritual and a political function in society. In some areas the church has all but abandoned political responsibility to the community.

Congregation Had a Political Function

The New Testament adopted a Greek word, *ekklesia,* for the church that had a political meaning. During the city-state era of Greek history *ekklesia* was used for the regularly summoned assembly of certain citizens charged with caring for the affairs of the city (state). At the cry of the Herald, the selected citizens would separate themselves from others and assemble at the meeting place ready to do the business of the community. Somewhere in the process of time, the church lost several aspects of the root meaning. This could be the primary cause for the lack of Christian action in relation to the current ethical and moral warfare. Church was not to be just a "place;" it was to be "people" assembled for worship, then scattered to share the good news.

Aid and Comfort to the Enemies of Christ

The selective nature of the called out ones has been abandoned. The aspect of separation from others to do special work has been minimized along with the idea of special leadership roles which must function to protect the community. The meeting house has been neglected and in some cases actually abandoned. The spiritual responsibility for others has been abdicated or delegated to a paid staff. The concern for the welfare of the "City" has been discarded for the spirit of laissez-faire (non-interference with the action of individuals). Such indifference becomes an aid and comfort to the enemies of Christ and weakens the church's ability to defend the fortress of faith.

All these essential elements of *ekklesia* were included in what the Greek version of the Old Testament called the assembly of Israel. The Septuagint used *ekklesia* to explain its function. These basic ideas were incorporated in the early gathering of the believers and caused the word *ekklesia* to be used. Why is there little effort to maintain the essential function of the church?

A Colony of Kindred Souls

The gathered church has been compared to a colony of people in a strange land but not part of the land. What scripture called, "in the world, but not of the world." A colony is a group living in a location other than their homeland, but remaining under the control of the home country and maintaining all the customs and lifestyle of their homeland.

Peter saw the early church "as strangers and sojourners" Such citizens of the kingdom living in a hostile world, gathered themselves in congregations much like a fort and were bound together similar to the rules that govern a colony. They were kindred minds joined in heart to bring the message and lifestyle of the homeland to the new but hostile land. By establishing colonies, compounds and forts to protect themselves, the church became something of a city-state equipped both to protect the members and to carry the good news to the population of the hostile land.

> 9. But you are a chosen race, a royal priesthood, a dedicated nation, and a people God means to have for Himself, that you might show forth His praises who called you out of darkness into His amazing light. 10. There was a time when you were not a people, now you are God's people because you obtained mercy. 11. Beloved, I urge you, as strangers and sojourners, to abstain from the physical desires, which battle against the soul. (1 Peter 2:9-11 EDNT)

Esprit de corps

The gathered church cannot expect the existing system of education or any other government program to serve as an adequate catalyst for a moral renaissance. Spiritual heroes, with contagious esprit de corps, are required to effect moral change. Spiritual leadership knows the church is the last line of defense for the family, the community, and the cause of ethics and morality in the nation. Somehow the local congregation must recapture the Esprit de corps that existed in first century Christianity.

Among the early believers there was a spirit of defensive concern, aggressively displayed, for the corporate honor and interests of the group with particular concern for each member of the body. Each individual was willing to resist unto death for the cause. It is from this willingness to die that we get the true understanding of martyrdom. Simon Peter's response to the betrayal of Jesus at Gethsemane was typical of the spirit of the early brotherhood. When Judas came with a large company of religious leaders and elders of the city, Peter drew his sword and attacked. Out numbered, Peter went for a head and got an ear instead, but the spirit of resistance was there. This willingness of one sword against a mob typifies the Esprit de corps of the early believers.

Martyrdom came about because an individual's lifestyle led to the risk of personal safety and security coupled ultimately with the willingness to give up life itself for the Cause. The early Greek use of *martyr* and the present concept included in the word "witness" share the same root source and meaning. To affect renewal, the church must have committed individuals with a lifestyle that functions as an active witness in defense of the Christian cause. Such a willingness to confront contemporary culture when it violates basic ethical and moral standards would identify the areas of concern and bring public pressure on offensive conduct. Should this not affect the necessary change, the next step would need to be more militant.

The Experience Base

The testing ground of experience makes it clear that it is most difficult to change society as a whole. Individuals change more easily that do groups; groups change more easily than organizations, and organizations change more easily that society. Since it is difficult to change even one individual, it takes great concerted effort by large numbers to effect significant change; however, this change is still one person at a time. The local congregation has the experience base, in one-on-one evangelism, to effect this change in society. Can believers muster the heart and kindred spirit to challenge the enemy on hostile turf?

Deep in the Old Testament, Jeremiah cried that God would make a covenant with His people:

> "I will put my law in their inward parts, and write it in their hearts; and will be their God, and they shall be my people." (Jeremiah 31:330 b)

Paul spoke again of the inclusion of Gentiles:

> 22. What if God, willing to display His anger, and to make His power known, was patient and long-suffering with vessels of wrath prepared for destruction: 23. and did so that He might make known the full value of the vessels prepared for compassion, which He made ready beforehand, 24. even us, whom He has called, not the Jews only, but also the Gentiles? 25. As He said also in the Book of Hosea, Those who were not My people I will call My people; and she who was not beloved, I will call My beloved. 26. And in the same place where they were told, You are not My people; there they will be called the children of the living God. 27. And Isaiah proclaimed aloud concerning Israel, Although the number of the children of Israel is as the sand of His work on the earth, and justly cut it short. 28. for the Lord will consummate His work on the earth, and justly cut it short. (Romans 9:24-28 EDNT)

Joined in Heart

Prayer is one of the common bonds that join believers in mind and heart. Each individual Christian must see themselves as part of the team. Jesus sent out the early disciples two by two. When the disciples asked Jesus to teach them to pray, they did not ask <u>how</u> to pray or <u>when</u> to pray; they asked him "Teach *us* to pray."

> 1. As Jesus ceased praying in a certain place, one of His disciples asked, Lord, teach us to pray, as John taught his disciples. 2. And Jesus said, When you pray say, Our Father, may your name be honored. Your reign begin, your will be done in Heaven and on earth. 3. Continue giving us daily the food we need. 4. And forgive our sins; for we too forgive all who are indebted to us. And keep us clear of temptation, and rescue us from evil. (Luke 11:1-4 EDNT)

One should notice the plural nature of the Lords Prayer. The disciples said, "Lord teach *us* to pray." Have you noticed the plural pronouns? They were to pray *our* Father, give *us* day by day, forgive *us*, lead *us*, and deliver *us*. The model of the Lords Prayer begins with adoration for God, continues with an acknowledgment of our subjection to God's will, asks petitions of God, and ends with an ascription of praise; an acknowledgment that God has all power in heaven and in earth.

It remains for each of us to adjust our minds and hearts to the circumstances. The Lords Prayer suggested the disciples may need assistance with daily bread, that there would be the occasion of sin, that there could be transgressions against us by others, and that there would be the ever present temptation and the need for deliverance from evil. It also suggested that God had the power to provide deliverance from these ever-present difficulties. So in the process of adjusting our mind and heart we must also tap into God's source of power, which renewed spirit within us that makes us different. This power will assist us in fighting all the little Amalekites that plague the world.

Certainly there is strength in the company of the committed, but individuals must be prepared to resist Satan and the forces of evil on a personal basis. One individual believer and God can be a majority against personal attacks, but do not confuse individual attacks of the devil against lone believers as the only problem; there are coordinated attacks of evil forces against the gathered church: this is spiritual warfare in the most dangerous form. When individuals are weakened through personal attacks, they are not readily available to come to the rescue of others. Individual Christians have a responsibility to remain strong and available to assist in the defense of the group. Peter as an old and wise man gave good advice to believers:

6. Bow down before the strong hand of God, that in His good time He may lift you up. 7. Throw back on Him the burden of your anxiety; because He cares for you. 8. Have a thoughtful demeanor, be on guard, because your enemy the devil, prowls about as an angry lion, seeking someone to greedily consume. 9. Be strong in faith and stand up to the devil, knowing that you share the same suffering with your brothers all over the world. 10. And the God of all grace who has called us to enjoy His eternal glory in Christ Jesus, after you suffer a little He will restore, strengthen, and establish you as a resident of heaven. 11. To Him be glory and power through endless ages, Amen. (1 Peter 5:6-11 EDNT)

Kindred Minds

Paul, the Apostle, wanted each believer to maintain "the mind of Christ" (Philippians 2:5-11) and to keep kindred minds joined in heart for each circumstance. Perhaps a look at the viewpoints of Jesus during various circumstances of his life would provide a pattern for handling difficulties. Jesus was presented in the Gospels as a man of action. A man who went about doing good. Having done well in one place, Jesus immediately would go on to another circumstance where he again was of a mind to do good.

Jesus in the Temple

First, let's look at Jesus at age twelve in the Temple. While others were traveling with the caravan back to their comfortable homes, Jesus as a lad of twelve was in the Temple discussing spiritual things with the leaders of the Temple. When Jesus was asked the reason for His presence in the Temple, the answer was clear, "I must be about my Father's business" (Luke 2:39-52).

Fasting and Prayer in the Wilderness

Another occasion when Jesus faced overwhelming difficulty, he elected to fast and pray for an extended period. In this physically weakened condition, Satan tempted him (Mark 1:12,13; Luke 4:1-13). The scripture says that Jesus was tempted in all manner like as we are yet without sin (Hebrews 4:15). The question is, how did Jesus overcome temptation? Well, obviously there was commitment, fasting, prayer, but he also used the Word of God. Jesus used the Word of God to overcome Satan's temptation. Could we not do the same to adjust our attitude and fly above the storm?

Prayer in the Garden

Another important occasion in the life of Christ was the occasion of his prayer in the Garden of Gethsemane when he was making preparation for the cross (Luke 22:39-46). He prayed, "Father, not my will but thine be done." This prayer of relinquishment where His will was brought under submission to the will of the Father is a good example for an ongoing process that works. Your mind and heart can be changed for the better.

After Jesus had completed the mission the Father had sent Him to do, and He had sent His disciples to continue His work, He prayed to the Father from the cross, "Into thy hands I commend my spirit." Then He gave the ultimate declaration about the work of salvation. He said, "It is finished" (John 19:30). When an individual accepts the saving grace of Jesus Christ and submits his spirit to the redirection of the Holy Spirit, the work of salvation may be finished but the process of living has just begun. It will take many adjustments in the mind and hearts of individual believers to maintain the right attitude towards God and the proper angle against the contrary wind in order to fly above the storm.

Power in Heaven

Remember, Jesus is in a present position of power. He is at the right hand of the Father. His purpose there is to intercede or mediate between God and man. When Jesus stood in Heaven as the young Deacon Stephen was adjusting his mind and heart to the stoning and opposing wind of his day, it must have thrilled the very heart of Jesus to hear Stephen pray, "Lord, lay not this sin to their charge" (Acts 7:60). Certainly, this was Christ-like. Stephen won that last battle of bigotry and hatred. He had the capacity to forgive and pray for those who despitefully used him to work out their own frustration.

Surely Stephen had exercised the mind of Christ for it was on the cross where Jesus forgave those who crucified him. Not only at the moment of death as in the case of Stephen, but throughout life each believer must constantly adjust his mind and heart so that the mind of Christ would be demonstrated by actions. Reminded of the film "Cool Hand Luke" where the star was punished severely for each transgression until he "got his mind right!" As each believer is humbled to the place they can say, "I got my mind right!" much can be accomplished in the fight for right. With this accomplishment, each individual will be armed with heavenly weapons and may overcome the powers of darkness. The battle belongs to the Lord, but believers must be armed with watchful care.

A Gathering of Strangers

A mobilization of workers for the military manufacturing during World War II changed the face of the church. Prior to this period of history, the congregation was homogeneous, a gathering of family and friends. With similar interests and common beliefs, the membership was harmonious. They lived in the same community, went to the same schools, shopped in the same stores, and worked in the same places. Their politics and their morality were common and protected, but the circumstance of the local congregation has changed.

During the great mobilization, places of worship became a gathering of strangers and it remains so in most areas. The gathered church is no longer just family and friends, it is filled with strangers. The busy program schedule does not necessarily bind the congregation together. About the time the strangers begin to fit in, their company moves them again. People who have been with the congregation for years are transferred and more strangers move in to take their place.

Also, the leader is no longer one of the "home boys," but comes from another state and a different subculture. This has complicated the readiness and effectiveness of individual believers to do battle with the enemies of Christianity. These changes in the temperament of the congregation require that each member be more alert and armed with watchful care. The concept of "readiness" is to be equipped and prepared to resist attacks and care for the fallen.

> 1. Let every person line up under governing authorities. For all authority comes from God: the existing authorities have been established by God. 2. Whoever therefore resists authority is opposing God's established order: they that resist will bring judgment on themselves. 3. Those with good conduct have nothing to fear because established authorities are against the wrongdoer. Do you want to have no fear of authorities? Then do what is good, and you will receive praise: 4. for the magistrate is the minister of God to you for good. But if you do wrong, you have reason to be alarmed; for the sword of justice is not without meaning: for the magistrates are the ministers of God to execute punishment to the evil doer. 5. Therefore you must line up under authority, not only to escape God's anger, but also because it is the right thing to do. 6. For this cause also pay your taxes: for the authorities are God's ministers, devoting themselves to this work. 7. Pay what you owe: taxes to whom taxes are due; custom duties

to whom payment is due; look at and pay attention to those entitled to respect; honor to those entitled to honor. 8. Leave no debt unpaid, except the debt of love to others: for he who loves his neighbor has done what the law demands. 9. The commandments are: You must not adulterate your vows, You must not murder, You must not steal, You must not desire what others have, and if there be any other commandment, it simply means, You shall love your neighbor as yourself. 10. Love does not intentionally do wrong to a neighbor: love, therefore, satisfies the law completely. 11. The time is now that you must awake to reality: for salvation is nearer than when we first believed. 12. The night is almost over and dawn is near: let us therefore lay aside the clothing of the night, and put on the weapons of light. 13. Let us behave honestly in the day light; not in partying and intoxicated behavior, not in secret places of immorality, not in conflict and greed. 14. But clothe yourselves with the Lord Jesus Christ, and make no plans to fulfill the desires of the flesh. (Romans 13:1-14 EDNT)

CHAPTER FIVE

Armed With Watchful Care

> In heavenly armor we'll enter the land,
> No weapon that's fashioned against us will stand,
> When the power of darkness comes in like a flood,
> He's raised up a standard, the pow'r of His blood,
> The battle belongs to the Lord.
>
> - Jamie Owens-Collins -

Brace and Await Orders

During a morning worship service in Atlanta, a young man stood up abruptly, braced at attention, and remained rigid for a few moments. After the service he came forward and apologized for disrupting the service. He was assured that it was OK. His explanation for acting in the abrupt manner was revealing.

It was during the Vietnam War and he had just spent four years in the US Marine Corps. He was accustomed to standing at attention when an officer entered the room. His explanation was simple, "Sir, I felt the presence of a Superior Officer and didn't know anything to do but brace and await orders!" It would be marvelous were the Presence of God strong enough and believers sufficiently disciplined to recognize God's Presence and brace and await orders. The battle would certainly be joined and the victory assured.

Coming to attention military style is called "bracing." The word clearly means support, strengthen, or hold steady. Such a posture prepares the soldier for a struggle, impact, or danger and suggests a readiness to follow orders. We need a Together/Strong Network that will be aware of God's Presence and be ready to act at His command.

Together/Strong Network for the Faithful

Early Christians, when they witnessed the struggle or suffering of colleagues, acted to express their common "feelings with" their fellows. The early believers seemed to have an understanding of mutual and parallel susceptibility to the evil conditions that prevailed. As early Christians expressed their concern for one another, they created the first together-strong network and fortified themselves against the onslaughts of evil.

The ancient Greeks, in whose language the New Testament was written, discovered that if a person really cared about the circumstances of his fellow, he might enter vicariously into that person's experience. They called this *sympathos,* meaning *with suffering,* from which comes the English word sympathy. By means of sympathy one enters into the minds and hearts of those who struggle or suffer, to share their burdens.

The old Latins, in whose language most of the history of the early church was written, discovered that when sympathy was sincere, a miracle resulted among the supported. They called it *comfortis,* meaning *together strong,* and from it comes the present word "comfort."

The local congregation should be a true together/strong network of loving and supporting friends united against a common foe. The battle belongs to the Lord, but the local congregation must organize a resistance and maintain a vigil against attacks from evil forces. This means that each individual believer must be armed and prepared for battle. It also means that care and concern must be demonstrated for those who stumble or fall as the battle is joined against evil. Each believer must be a good soldier.

If the congregation is to be strong and effective it must have leadership that has been nurtured and supported along the way. All who have attained positions of responsibility and leadership in the Christian movement will respond in unison that they could not make it without the support of the body of believers. It is this kind of support group that is required to resist the forces of evil that come against believers.

Jesus Himself was an emotional man who wanted others around Him for encouragement. One lonely question in the New Testament underscores this when Jesus asked of His closest followers, "Could you not watch with me one hour?" Believers are no less dependent on the watchful care of others. To effectively protect each other and the group, Christians must use all the weapons in God's armory. With the heavenly armor and spiritual weapons believers can find strength to resist the cunning propaganda and tactics of the devil.

Paul in Ephesians spoke of the whole armor of God. Believers were to use the strength of their maturity in Christ to proclaim the truthful message of grace, concealing nothing. They were to tell the whole story by life and lip without fear because of the protection of the armor.

Put on the Armor of God

A free translation of Paul's words in Ephesians would read: *Protect yourself with all of God's armor, then, you will be able to stand your ground when the evil times come, and be found still on your feet, when the entire task is over.* The Christian soldier was to bind the good message to their feet and be prepared to publish the gospel of peace. This would make their feet ready to take the field of battle. Their feet were to speak of their courage and determination to conquer the enemy.

Stand fast and guard yourself with the strength of the truth. This will put down all the doubts projected by the wicked. Take up the shield of faith, with it you will be able to quench all the fire-tipped arrows of your wicked enemy; Use your own helmet of salvation, one that fits your head securely and defends your head from all sides; this will bring you the assurance of final victory. Take the sword of God's Breath that He placed in Adam to make him a living soul. Take every word that proceeds out of the Mouth of God and march toward the enemy.

The early Christian soldier was told to earnestly worship at the time of each opportunity. And not to forsake the assembling together with the body. Paul warned: "Do not be AWOL at the time of roll call." Make your petitions known to the body, marshal a persistent attitude and action toward all your fellow soldiers. Be watchful! Pray for the leadership to speak clearly and boldly and declare the coded message meant only for the soldiers in the battle. Be silent at your induction or initiation. The battle is ahead. Save your energy for the fight. Let your light shine!

> 10. Finally, my brothers, be strengthened in the Lord, and in the power of His unlimited resource. 11. Wear the complete armor of God, so you can stand against the strategy and assault of the adversary. 12. For our wrestling is not against a physical enemy, but against evil princes of darkness who rule this world, against hosts of spiritual wickedness in heavenly warfare. 13. Wherefore wear the complete armor of God that you may be able to withstand evil attacks when they come, and be found still standing. 14. Stand your ground, being protected by Truth, and having integrity for a

breastplate; 15. and the gospel of peace preparing your feet for battle, 16. above all, take the shield of faith to extinguish all the fiery darts of the wicked. 17. And take the helmet, which is salvation, and the sword of the Spirit, which is the word of God: 18. praying on every occasion through petition in the Spirit, and be vigilant with unwearied perseverance and supplication for all saints; 19. and pray for me, that fluency of speech may be given me, that I may make known courageously the sacred secret of the gospel, (Ephesians 6:10-19 EDNT).

A Good Soldier

Paul had some additional words about Christian warfare and the good soldier:

> 1. My son, keep empowering yourself in the grace that is in Christ Jesus. 2. And entrust the things you learned from me which were confirmed by many witnesses, to faithful men who will be competent to teach others also. 3. Join the ranks of those who share hardships as a soldier of Jesus Christ. 4. No active warrior entangles himself with ordinary affairs; so he may please the one who enlisted him as a soldier. (2 Timothy 2:1-4 EDNT)

Moral Influence

The moral influence of religious leaders is at a low ebb. The whole world knows about the private sins of popular preachers and now it seems the whole world knows more that they want to know about the private lives and public sins of public leaders who profess to be Christian. What can be done to restore the integrity of spiritual leadership? How can we stand in the gap and pray and arm the congregation to care for those who have fallen prey to Satan's schemes?

The ministry of believers must include the edification of the family and friends. The gathering of believers is to be a sanctuary, a refuge for the troubled and sinful. Such a meeting is not a club for sinners, but it is a rehabilitation hospital for saints who have been wounded in the spiritual battles between good and evil.

Scripture is clear that believers are to restore those who fall into sin:

> 1. Brethren, if a man should make an unintended error due to weakness, you who are regenerated, repair and adjust him with a teachable spirit; continue considering yourself, lest you also be tempted to make a false step. 2. Practice in sharing the heavy burdens of others, and you will fulfill the principle of Christ. 3. If a man supposes himself to be something when he is really nothing, he deceives himself. 4. Let every man test himself for innocence, and then he shall rejoice in himself and not in another. 5. For every man must carry his own personal load. (Galatians 6:1-5 EDNT)

Take a look at "an unintended error" it literally means to be surprised that you are about to do something wrong, as if a child began to eat before permission. Normally one thinks of "overtaken in a fault" to mean restoration after the fact, but the verb used here literally means "to take before; to anticipate or forestall." It appears that the verb deals with prevention or stopping before the transgression. Again "restore" suggests restoration after the fact, because the word can mean "reconciling factions," but an important use of the word is to prepare a ship before it sails, or supply an army with provisions before a battle; this is anticipatory prevention. To instruct a believer when one observes an inclinations toward wrong doing and intervenes to prevent or alter the behavior. Guiding one to make a change before wrong doing is the best meaning of the verse. Prevention is easier than restoration.

No Novice in Battle

Leadership experience is required to adequately

resist Satan. No novice is to be sent into battle. There must be systematic and sustained training for new converts. Each recruit must be nourished and trained in the basic knowledge of behavior that is taught in the Word of God. Trained to protect himself and others in battle and trained to care for the wounded who have fallen in battle.

Assumptions for Rehabilitation

Paul made several assumptions about the brotherhood of believers. Assumptions were made that individuals could succumb to evil forces and become disconnected from the body of believers without proper instruction and training Even moral delinquency in the brotherhood should not cause others to feel superior. Paul also assumed that spiritual members of the group would work to prevent individuals from being separated from the brotherhood. It was clear that the process of restoration should be done early and be done with a teachable spirit where the individuals involved learned from the experience. Also, the knowledge gained in dealing with the process of restoration was to be a sobering awareness of each individual's own susceptibility to temptation. Those things learned, during the process, were to be taught to others to strengthen the body of believers against evil forces and prepare them to be soldiers in spiritual warfare.

Walk in the Spirit

In the closing of Galatians Chapter Five Paul discussed the works of the flesh and the Fruit of the Spirit.Clearly, Paul believed that believers should also walk in the Spirit.

> 18. But if you are guided by the Spirit, you no longer need to follow the law. 19. Now the behavior that belongs to the flesh is obvious, they are: (sensual sins) unfaithfulness in

marriage, unrestrained living, unbridled acts of indecency; 20.(religious sins) the worship of idols, the use of drugs and magical powers; (temperamental sins) hostility, strife, jealousy, violent flare-ups of temper, self-seeking ambitions, adherence to contradictory teaching; 21.(personal sins) desires to appropriate what others have, drunkenness and carousing, and similar things: I warned you before that people who do such things will have no part in the kingdom of God. (Galatians 5:18-21 EDNT)

The concept of "walking" in scripture normally refers to one's daily activities and attitudes. The Apostle was firm that the idea of "love" should be the controlling factor in the relationship of believers. The law of love allows for degrees of difference on both sides of an issue. It is clear that good cannot totally withstand bad and that badness within the brotherhood must not suppress good will and good deeds.

There is no logical chapter break here, because Chapter Six begins with the idea of Christian brotherhood and mutual relationship with Christ. This true brotherhood is to feel responsible for each other and to take measures to maintain the level of spiritual fellowship sufficient to perpetuate the law of love in Christ. Paul acknowledged with affectionate admonition that some of the brethren could be "overtaken" by the evil forces in the world and the goal of the brotherhood should be prevention first and urgent restoration to the straight and narrow way. There were no exceptions: prevention and restoration was available to all through the action of the "spiritual ones."

Obligation of Rehabilitation

Restore is a medical concept and here suggests the setting of a dislocated bone. When temptation comes to an individual they often become "dislocated" and feel great discomfort. Treatment must be personal and immediate. Full restoration normally will not come without the assistance of others. The group is obligated by the opportunity to first prevent and then restore those caught in the snare of evil.

Just as one would not take lightly the effort to set a broken bone or a dislocated shoulder, careful consideration and preparation must be taken to bring about restoration, but to caution the individual and prevent the fall would be better. Normally, the task of setting a bone is not given to a novice or an untrained person. Likewise, those responsible for restoring "dislocated" individuals in the brotherhood must have special character and skills.

Persons Authorized to Restore

The business of recovery and restoration of a fallen member requires individuals with spiritual qualifications and sufficient awareness of evil to adequately resist temptation. The genuinely spiritual individual manifests the fruit of the Spirit: love. The task of restoration of those caught in the wiles of Satan belongs to the spiritual ones who are led by the Holy Spirit. There must be no judging of individual behavior, even the most spiritual are subject to temptation.

It is the responsibility of the group to restore. Those who seek to restore must not attempt to punish. When God forgives, the congregation must forgive. In the past some groups have "shot the wounded." Care must be taken to love the sinner even when the sin is hated. The total concern must be prevention and restoration.

Restoration is a group concern although it may be affected by individuals. Here Paul changes from the plural reference to the group for restoration to the singular idea of concern for the individual involved in the process of restoration. Each one involved in restoring a fallen comrade must be aware that they are vulnerable themselves to the same kind of sin. Paul was concerned for these personal liabilities and vulnerabilities. This awareness must be a significant part of the preparation to participate in rescuing a wounded brother from the clutches of the enemy.

Ask any first aide person about the risks of rescue whether at the scene of an accident or on the battlefield. The group cannot adequately protect the individual from encounters with evil. Each believer must "Bear his own burden" and assume personal responsibility, not only for preparedness, but also for private acts.

Simon Peter is a good bad example of how a committed individual can be tempted when he is alone and some distance from the group. He followed Jesus closely for three years and boasted an overconfident attitude, but cursed, lied and denied Christ on the day of the Crucifixion. Yet, the Angel at the Tomb told the women, "Go your way, tell his disciples and Peter." Those words, "and Peter," spoke volumes about Christ's concern for the restoration of Peter. (Mark 16:7)

Spirit of Restoration

Believers are told to restore in the spirit of meekness and to consider themselves susceptible to temptation. Meekness suggests a teachable spirit that benefits from the experience. Working with others who have fallen to the forces of evil fortifies one to resist temptation. Knowing the consequence of certain behavior is the greatest prohibition to wrong action. Scripture is clear that we learn about Satan's deceptive devices from the mistakes of others.

> 11. Now all these things happened to them as examples and are written for our warning, and judgment has come to the

heirs of wrath. 12. Wherefore let him who thinks he stands today take heed that he does not fall tomorrow. 13. No test has come your way but such as is common to man: God is faithful, who will not permit you to be tempted beyond your endurance; but will with each test also show you a way of escape, so that you may be victorious. (1 Corinthians 10:11-13 EDNT).

11. Lest Satan outsmart us: for we know of his schemes (2 Corinthians 2:11 EDNT).

Attitude Controlling the Process

Believers are told to bear one another's burdens in order to fulfill the law of Christ. A humble spirit is also required to keep an individual from being deceived about personal value and to reinforce an individual need for spiritual resources. There is an individual responsibility for the process. Each individual must test their part of the process. The best way to do this is to teach others what has been learned and thereby strengthen the body of believers against Satan's devices.

The primary lesson learned from the process is the law of the harvest (sowing and reaping). Those involved in the process of restoration become more aware that one reaps not only what is sown, but that the evil seeds multiply and the evil harvest is usually worse than could be expected. From small indiscretions come large consequences.

12. Blood-related* and fortunate is the man who flinches not under the enticement of testing: for when he is proved trustworthy, he shall be given the wreath of honor that verifies vitality, which God promised to all who worship out of a benevolent heart. 13. Let no man say when he is enticed, God allured me to evil: for God does not use wickedness to validate the trustworthiness of any man. 14. But every man is attracted to wicked deeds, when he chooses action

based on personal desire, and hope of pleasure. 15. Then when personal desire has joined together with enticement, it produces a voluntary transgression: and this offense produces separation from observant morality, and at the end separation from God. 16 . Do not wander from the right or deviate from the true course, my cherished band of brothers. (James 1:12-16 EDNT)

---

* v12 To bless, in Middle English used at the time of KJV, had a meaning related to "blood" used to consecrate an altar; thus, the use of "blood-related."

The fallen may be restored by the spiritual ones. This is to be done in a spirit of teachableness with the restorer careful to guard against temptation. To complete the process of restoration, the places of worship and the objects of ministry must be cleansed and anointed again for God's Holy purpose.

A Plan for Restoration

When a person in spiritual leadership fails, and the sin is known, it becomes necessary to re-consecrate the places and instruments of worship the leader violated during the period of un-confessed sins. This should be done with the knowledge and consent of the faithful who remain responsible for the worship of God in the particular place and the ongoing spiritual service to mankind. By their consent and knowledge and they are participants in the process and receive spiritual healing. The process should restore confidence in both the place and the persons involved in ministry.

As the furnishings of the Tabernacle in the Old Testament were anointed with oil, action may need to be taken in the congregation. After a general prayer for the assistance of the Holy Spirit, use anointing oil (representing the Holy Spirit) on the tip of a finger and make the sign of the Cross on windows and doors in the building and rooms and offices used by the person who violated the sacred trust of the people. Repeating at each sign of the Cross: "By the authority of Jesus Christ and by the cleansing power of His blood, I bind and cast out any evil or demonic powers and send them to the place appointed by Jesus." (Luke 9:1; Luke 10:17). In the sanctuary, place the sign of the Cross with oil on top of the pulpit and on the front and sides of the pulpit. Do the same for the pulpit Bible and other instruments normally used in worship.

The reason the windows, doors, pulpit, and pulpit Bible are anointed is to sanctify and protect those places from evil or from the return of evil spirits. The scriptures are full of anointing: the most vivid is the angel of death passing over the first born of each Jewish household when the blood of the lamb was put on the two door posts. (Exodus 12:7). Jesus' blood once and for all time cleanses us and gives us the victory over sin and death.

> 57. But thanks to God, who gives us the victory through our Lord Jesus Christ. 58. Therefore, my beloved, be unwavering, holding your ground and always flourishing in the work of the Lord, forasmuch as you know that your hard work is always fruitful in the Lord. (1 Corinthians 15:57 EDNT)

Stand Against the Strategy and Assault of the Adversary

> 10. Finally, my brothers, be strengthened in the Lord, and in the power of His unlimited resource. 11. Wear the complete armor of God, so you can stand against the strategy and assault of the adversary. 12. For our wrestling is not against a physical enemy, but against evil princes of darkness who rule this world, against hosts of spiritual wickedness in heavenly warfare. 13. Wherefore wear the complete armor of God that you may be able to withstand evil attacks when

they come, and be found still standing. 14. Stand your ground, being protected by Truth, and having integrity for a breastplate; 15. and the gospel of peace preparing your feet for battle, 16. above all, take the shield of faith to extinguish all the fiery darts of the wicked. 17. And take the helmet, which is salvation, and the sword of the Spirit, which is the word of God: 18. praying on every occasion through petition in the Spirit, and be vigilant with unwearied perseverance and supplication for all saints; 19. and pray for me, that fluency of speech may be given me, that I may make known courageously the sacred secret of the gospel, 20. for which I am an envoy in a coupling-chain bound to a guard: that in spite of that detail I may speak bravely, as I ought to speak. (Ephesians 6:10-20 EDNT)

CHAPTER SIX

Storming The Ramparts

Sure I must fight if I would reign -
Increase; my courage, Lord!
I'll bear the toil, endure the pain,
Supported by Thy Word.

- Isaac Watts -

Somewhere Listening for My Name

A young man was working in the Chapel garden at Oxford Graduate School. He was told to work quietly, because it was a sacred place and that God might speak to him while he was near the chapel. The garden is below the high wall of the chapel court. Standing at the high wall and Travis working slowly below, I asked, "Travis, what are you doing?" He was surprised and startled. Later, he explained "I was thinking, what if God speaks to me? What will I say? Suddenly, I heard my name…'TRAVIS' from above…I thought God was calling my name." What if we were all sensitive to the voice of God? Out of the past from a more spiritual generation comes the words of an old song, "I'll be somewhere working….I'll be somewhere listening for my name."

Spilled Ink, a Skunk, and a Troubled Soldier

Traveling to Washington, DC during the Vietnam War to intercede for a young service man that experienced discrimination because of his faith, God opened a door for witness. Just before catching the plane, my schedule took me to a publisher to review the galley proof of a book. While there an old newspaper was noticed on the floor. Since neatness is a virtue, my decision was to pick up the paper. It had been used to cover an ink spill and was stuck to the floor. In the process, a small piece tore off in my hand. It was a picture of a skunk and a story about a farmer.

A Pennsylvania farmer had observed an old skunk for several days. One day the skunk abandoned his old home and dug a new nesting hole. The farmer was intrigued, so he watched. The skunk with great care gathered grass and leaves and lined the inside of the excavation. The skunk looked around for what was to be his last glance at the world, and then entered the hole. The behavior fascinated the farmer so he waited. When the skunk never came out of the hole, the farmer became curious.

Taking a stick, the farmer punched into the hole. Nothing happened. Finally, he knelt down and raked back the leaves so the skunk could be seen. The skunk did not move; it was dead. The farmer observed that the skunk was old, the teeth were broken, and concluded the skunk could no longer hunt for food and had prepared to die. Reading this story seemed foolish at the time, but God had a reason.

Seated about half way back in the coach section, a young soldier chose the empty seat beside me. As the plane took off, the soldier turned and said, "I probably won't be alive a year from now, I'm on my way to Vietnam." This matter of fact statement jolted my memory of the skunk story. As the story was shared with the young soldier, his face became thoughtful. The time had come for me to present the claims of Christ. If an old skunk had enough sense to prepare to die, surely it would be wise for a soldier going to battle to make preparation to die. His answer, "Sir, I would if I knew how."

The door was wide open. The ABC's of the gospel (all have sinned, believe on the Lord Jesus Christ, and confess with your mouth and you will be saved.) were presented. The young soldier prayed to receive Christ and went to war prepared to die. God uses spilled ink, old newspapers, a plane ride, and a troubled but searching heart to do the work of redemption.

A Winning Attitude

Attitude is a predisposition to act. When the enemy is at the gate and the command is to storm the ramparts, a winning attitude is needed to move forward. When the enemy comes in like a flood and the defenders are falling to the right and to the left, it is difficult to remember that the battle is the Lord's. Without total trust in the Commander, it is difficult to keep confidence in the outcome. At such times a simple adjustment may be required in your predisposition to act responsibly in face of the enemy. Some call this "courage". We need more spiritual courage.

Attitude and Action

Attitude and action are closely related, in fact, action changes your attitude. It is not possible to change your feeling simply by changing your mind. The change must be based on faith and faith requires action. In reality it is the action or the act of faith that causes the change in outlook and the consequent change in feeling. The nature of life requires constant adjustment in ones perception of the ultimate outcome of any difficulty. It is the abiding presence of God that provides confidence during the bitter battles against evil. Jesus said,

> 23. Jesus answered, Those who love Me will keep My word: and My Father will love them, and we will dwell with them. (John 14:23 EDNT)

When duty requires the presentation of one's body as a sacrifice in the battle, the scripture is clear that one must be transformed by the renewing of the mind. To be a good soldier one must not be conformed to this world, but by attitude and action prove what is good and acceptable to God.

> 1. I implore you, brethren, by the compassions of God that you place yourselves as a living sacrifice, consecrated and pleasing to God, which is your reasonable worship. 2. And be not fashioned according to this age: but be transformed by a new mental attitude, that you may confirm for yourselves what is good, acceptable, and the complete will of God. (Romans 12:1, 2 EDNT)

Acting upon Faith

Most people in the world talk about the enemy, the difficulties, the problems, rather than attempt to storm the ramparts. It is not the talk about the battle, but the action toward winning that brings victory in all of life's spiritual adversities. Abraham, in the Old Testament, had hope against hope. He was able to adjust to the situation, stretch himself, and still believe God and act upon faith. Acting upon faith brought great assurance and hope. Abraham had stormed the ramparts and overcome the enemy. (Genesis 12:1-20)

Abraham left the Ur of Chaldees with his family to journey to the land of Canaan, but his family and baggage slowed him down and finally stopped him on his journey. Following the death of his father, God spoke to Abraham and prompted him to continue his journey. "Get thee out of thy country, and from thy kindred, and from thy father's house unto a land that I will show you." God prompted, but promised blessing with obedience. Willing to obey God, Abraham continued his journey.

Obedience and Action

Obedience and action seem to be the keys in the life of Abraham. Abraham was able to get the end result of his life straight with God and clear in his mind; consequently, he would not let individual circumstance rob him of obedience and praise. Abraham knew the battle plan that God had scheduled for his life. He understood God's promise, God's commands and God's covenants. He acted on them and became a man of both faith and hope. Take a quick look back to a time when Abraham had to take action to make a major adjustment in his attitude.

Early in the book of Genesis (Genesis 15:1-6), Abraham had a vision and heard God declare that He would be Abraham's shield from danger and would give him a great reward. Abraham's answer was, "God, what good will that do; I don't have any children, my only heir is a servant's son, you've given me no children of my own to inherit my property." When God spoke Abraham was dwelling in a black goatskin tent, and was most likely sitting on a three-legged stool staring at the barren earth. No wonder he had a poor attitude.

God said, "Abraham, go outside your tent. Look toward Heaven and count the stars, if you can. You will have that many descendants upon the earth." Of course, Abraham could not count all the stars. It dawned on him that his posterity would be numberless, so he adjusted his attitude and began to stretch himself because of the promises of God. Abraham had confidence in God's plan, but he was still tested. Acting on the Word of God does not mean that an individual will not have personal hardships to overcome. This was not the only time that God required Abraham to storm the ramparts of the enemy that required a personal test of will and faith.

There was an occasion when God spoke to Abraham and commanded him to make a sacrifice of his son, Isaac, (Genesis 22:1-19), as a token of his total commitment to the sovereignty and steadfastness of God. Knowing that he was to be the father of many nations, Abraham had the assurance that God would work out the technicalities of the situation within the framework of His promise and covenant. Therefore, by faith Abraham adjusted his attitude, acted upon his faith and stretched his confidence in God. Abraham did not argue, he did not question, he simply stormed the ramparts and won a personal victory. As a father he had to stretch himself considerably to incorporate this action into his humanity, but his act of faith was rewarded. Abraham is not alone in this human struggle between good and evil which requires one to adjust attitudes and actions to the higher will of God.

Look again at Abraham's story and follow him from the human perspective and see the nature of Abraham's attitude and the things that must have taken place in his mind and emotions. When Abraham got near the place of sacrifice and saw it in the distance, he spoke to the servants and required that they remain behind. But look at what he said, "The boy and I will go over there and worship, and then _we_ will come back to you." You see the faith of Abraham? He knew that God was in control. Complete obedience was the right action. Abraham was ready to storm the ramparts with total confidence in God's ultimate victory.

Abraham and his son began to climb the hill of difficulty and sacrifice. Isaac carried the wood for the sacrifice, and Abraham carried the knife and the coals for the fire. As they walked together the son questioned his father. Isaac asked, "I see that you have the coals and the wood for the fire, but where is the lamb for the sacrifice?" Look at Abraham stretch as he answers, "God himself will provide the sacrifice." As they walk together to the place of sacrifice, each step must have been a stretching experience for Abraham and a learning experience for Isaac.

Confidence and Obedience

With full confidence and complete obedience to God's voice, Abraham again heard from heaven. The Angel of the Lord said, "Now I know that you have complete obedience and reverence for God, because you would not withhold your only son from him." Abraham looked around and saw a ram caught in a bush by its horns. God had provided the sacrifice. Abraham's faith in God and confidence in the future was intact. God had been honored. Abraham had stormed the ramparts; the battle had been won. Abraham had overcome the barricades by prompt obedience. The right action had brought victory and hope.

The Battles are Different

The writer of Hebrews reminds believers that they "have not yet resisted unto blood, striving against sin." (Hebrews 12:4) God may not ask present day believers to make such an ultimate sacrifice as was required of Abraham. The present battles are not the same as the fight for Truth of the Crusaders in history. The current tactics of Satan does not normally include the giving of one's life in martyrdom, but there are still battles.

Some missionaries are still in harms way and some still sacrifice their lives on foreign soil, but most trials that come to present day Christians will be minor compared to the scriptural and historical record of those tests and trials that came to believers. Yet, there will be battles in the spiritual warfare that will require the full armor of God. All will face the hill of difficulty and the lions that guard the gate to victory, but just as Christian in his progress as a pilgrim, the ramparts of evil must be stormed and the gates of Hell must be challenged. When the right action is taken, we will discover that the enemy is powerless against the heavenly armor.

One Soldiers Confidence

Maj. General Jerry R. Curry (US Army Retired) had an experience in Korea that speaks to this issue. As an experienced Christian officer, with a great deal of military combat experience, he demonstrated both faith in God and confidence that his fellow soldiers could win the victory. On one occasion his troops were surrounded by enemy forces, with little hope of breaking out and no chance of reinforcements fighting their way in to rescue them. He sent a radio message for the artillery to blast a hole in the enemy circle at a given time. "Where do you want the bombardment?" Thinking the enemy might be listening, he told the man to remember the "Star of Bethlehem." The bombardment came in the East, on time and adequate for all the troops to escape.

This is an actual story of war, but the same could be true in the spiritual warfare. We must bring the knowledge learned for spiritual leaders into the daily battle. If we are strong and brave, call for assistance and have confidence in fellow soldiers of the Cross, the ultimate victory can be won. We can stand in the gap, believe and behave responsibly and give the next generation, if Jesus tarries, a chance to live the Christian life in a moral society.

A Point of Victory

Consider the successful businessman who overcame impossible odds through sustained faith in the

Word of God and arrived at a point of victory. He failed to secure a large expected contract. Saddened and disappointed he stormed the ramparts of disappointment and looked at his options. He could throw up his hands or he could change his attitude, stretch his faith, and take creative action. Instead of dwelling on the loss, he began to consider the possibilities. He called the company which had awarded the contract for equipment to someone else and suggested that his men were the finest installers in the area and requested the installation contract for the equipment. It was the right action and it led to over $2,000,000 of new business. He adjusted his attitude, he stretched his faith, he took the right action, and was blessed!

David and the Giant

The story of young David and the giant Goliath well illustrates the courage to storm the ramparts (1 Samuel 17:1-58). The Philistine Army was ready to destroy the Israelites. The Philistine Army included a family of giants. Goliath, the leader, was walking back and forth before the armies of Israel blaspheming the living God and threatening the destruction of God's people. Young David had come to the battlefield to see about the welfare of his brothers, and because of past experiences where God had delivered a bear and a lion into his hands as he protected his father's sheep, David felt confident and joyful that God was on his side.

David was a Volunteer

David volunteered to take on the Philistine giant with his slingshot, five smooth stones, and a heart of faith. Saul's armor was refused because David felt that he could face the giant with faith and a slingshot. He did not compare the giant's size to his own stature. David saw Goliath in terms of the size of God. He didn't think the giant was too big to hit. David knew the giant was too big to miss. Not only did David have the right attitude that had been stretched by his experience with the lion and the bear; consequently, he stormed the rampart of defeat and confronted the giant face to face. The evil giant that opposed God's people was defeated. David's attack honored his faith in God.

Although David was facing the champion of the camp of the Philistines who had defied the God of Israel, David was a volunteer. Goliath said, "If your volunteer wins and kills me we will be your slaves. But if I win and kill him you will be our slaves." So it was a challenge to the integrity of Israel's God. David took up that challenge, stretched his attitude and slung his sling. And God guided the stone.

Spiritual Lessons Learned

Goliath had challenged the army of Israel every morning and evening for forty days. The soldiers of Israel were terrified, they were intimidated, and they had become losers. David had learned some spiritual lessons. He had learned these lessons as the shepherd of his father's sheep, defending his flock against the bear and the lion. In these victories, David saw his effectiveness as a result of his faith and confidence in God. David was unafraid to challenge the giant in the name of God.

At first Saul, the King refused to let David fight Goliath saying, "You are just a boy and this man has been a soldier all his life." But David responded, "'I have taken care of my father's sheep and any time a lion or a bear carried off a lamb I would go after it, attack and rescue the lamb. And if the lion or bear turned on me I would grab it by the throat and beat it to death. I have killed lions and bears and I will do the same to this heathen Philistine who has defied the army of the living God. The Lord has saved me from the lions and the bears; He will save me from this Philistine." That is the attitude that makes one willing to storm the ramparts.

In the Name of the Lord

David's youth, equipment, and lack of military bearing insulted the giant. This was the appropriate action, evil should be insulted and challenged by people of faith. The giant threatened to feed David to the birds, but David answered, "You come against me with sword and spear, but I come against you in the name of the Lord Almighty. This very day the Lord will put you in my power; I will defeat you and cut off your head." As the giant walked toward him, David took a smooth stone out of his shepherd's bag and slung it at Goliath. It hit him on the forehead and broke his skull and Goliath fell face downward on the ground.

Victory without a Sword

So David, without a sword, defeated the giant with a sling and a stone. This was a great victory. David ran to him, stood upon him, took the giant's own sword and cut off his head. It took the right attitude, but it also required the right action. It may have taken a little adjustment and some stretching, but the action worked because it was the right action.

A Temporary Situation

As the armies of Israel, some people take the circumstances of life too seriously and do not take God seriously enough. Life itself is a temporary situation, so once we have put the end of life and our eternal destiny in the hand of God, how important could any given circumstance be? Nothing can really be a make or break situation when God is in control. So, if you want to take the right action, take God seriously. If you want to have the right attitude, do not take life too seriously. Do not let the circumstances of life control you. You can change your attitude, stretch your faith, and take control of your life by submitting to the power of God. You can act on your faith.

A Sunday school teacher was asked, "Why did David take five smooth stones with him, when there was only one giant? Was he afraid?" The teacher thought for a moment and answered, "Well, I guess David was prepared in case Goliath's brothers started any trouble."

A Young Bride

There is a story of a young bride who followed her husband to an army camp on the edge of a desert. The only living quarters she could find were primitive and near an Indian village. The heat was unbearable, and the wind blew constantly spreading sand everywhere.

The days were long and boring and the young woman's only neighbors were Indians. Her husband was away for several weeks at a time and her loneliness and the primitive living conditions almost got the best of her. So she called her mother and told her of the destitute circumstances and that she was returning home.

The mother's response was to share a story of two men in prison. "Two men were behind prison bars; one saw mud and the other saw stars." As the young bride thought on this statement, she began to consider the possibility that perhaps she should look around her - not at the difficulty, but at the opportunity. She lifted her eyes and began to look for the stars.

The young bride made friends with the Indians. In turn, they taught her weaving and pottery and returned her genuine interest with friendship. She became fascinated with the Indian culture, their history, and their way of life. She studied the desert and it began to change from a desolate, forbidding place to a marvelous thing of beauty. As she became excited about the possibilities, the days were no longer boring. She began to stretch and learn. She became an expert on that particular area of the desert and she wrote a book about it. What had changed? Not the desert, not the Indians. The young bride had changed her attitude; she had stretched herself and transformed a miserable experience into a rewarding life. She had stormed the ramparts of her fear, taken the right action and it worked wonders.

A Young Climber

A young climber with an experienced guide was camping high in the mountains. Early one morning a tremendous cracking sound suddenly awakened the young climber. He thought it was the end of the world. The guide explained that it was just the dawning of a new day. As the sun rose and thawed the ice, the melting caused movement and noise. The climber was told not to view the mountain from the previous sunset, but to see it clearly at sunrise. Are you guilty of viewing the circumstances of life as sunsets rather than the dawning of a new, bright opportunity? You must not let the failures of the past or the disappointments of the present discourage or defeat you. Accept the challenge of life's circumstances, ask God for what you want, or take what you get. Then, you can storm the ramparts and win.

Two Salesmen

Once there were two salesmen sent to an island to sell shoes. Riding a taxi in from the airport they noticed that no one on the island wore shoes. One became very discouraged and sent a telegram to his Home Office saying, "Am returning tomorrow. No one here wears shoes." A few minutes later the other salesman rushed into the telegraph office and sent this message, "Send 10,000 pairs of shoes. Everyone here needs shoes." The circumstances had not changed, but one man viewed the circumstances with optimism. One man adjusted his attitude and stretched his thinking. The other was defeated. Check the circumstance carefully; be sure you take the right action.

A Victory List

Perhaps you could keep a victory list as young David did. He knew and remembered his victories over the bears and the lions as he cared for his father's sheep. He also gave God the credit for those victories. Count your blessings, not your problems. Review your victory list during the difficult times. Keep your attitude in line with God's will. Then you can take the action that can bring victory and peace. You really don't need Saul's armor to face the giants and storm the ramparts in your life. Use what you have, adjust your attitude, take action, stretch yourself - in God - until you become adequate for the challenge. When God prompts...ACT!

When Believers Act

When believers act with a confident attitude at God's prompting, they will successfully storm the ramparts. As Christians develop kindred minds and are joined in heart with other believers, they are armed with a strong and prevailing faith. When they storm the ramparts of evil in their lives, an overcoming victory will surely come. As individuals develop a strategy against spiritual strongholds and push back the lingering spiritual darkness, God will surely give the victory over the forces of evil. The fight for the faith once delivered to the faithful saints must continue until every foe is vanquished, ever fallen comrade restored, and each martyr celebrated. Christ will then be the true Captain of Salvation and the battle will be the Lord's.

A Cloud of Witnesses

> 1. Therefore, since we are watched from above by such a cloud of witnesses, let us rid ourselves of all that weighs us down, and the sin that so persistently surrounds us, and let us run with steadfast endurance, the course that is marked out before us, 2. let this fix your eyes on Jesus the origin and the crown of all faith, who, to win His prize of blessedness, endured the cross and made light of its shame, Jesus, who now sits on the right of God's throne. 3. Consider Him who steadfastly endured such opposition at the hands of sinners, and compare your lives with His, so that you may not faint and grow weary in your souls. 4. you have not yet had to resist to the point of blood in your struggle against sin. (Hebrews 12:1-4 EDNT)

CHAPTER SEVEN
Soldiers Of The Cross

Stand up, stand up for Jesus,
Ye soldiers of the cross;
Lift high His royal banner,
It must not suffer loss: vict'ry unto vict'ry
His army shall He lead,
Till every foe is vanquished
And Christ is Lord indeed.

- George Duffield, Jr.-

Spiritual Warfare

Paul spoke to the Corinthians about the spiritual warfare that took place in the believer's mind:

> 3. Human beings we may be, but we do not fight our battles in human strength: 4. the weapons we use to fight are not human, but mighty through God to demolish strongholds; 5. casting down the conceits of men against the knowledge of God, and bringing every human thought into obedience to Christ; 6. when your submission reaches completion, I am prepared to settle all scores with the disobedient. (2 Corinthians 10:3-6 EDNT

Run, and not be Weary

Running they do not get weary and walking they do not fall by the wayside. Their strength is increased as they better understand the deliverance that comes only from God.

> 28 Hast thou not known? Hast thou not heard, that the everlasting God, the Lord, the Creator of the ends of the earth, fainteth not, neither is weary? There is no searching

of his understanding. 29 He giveth power to the faint; and to them that have no might he increaseth strength. 30 Even the youths shall faint and be weary, and the young men shall utterly fall: 31 But they that wait upon the Lord shall renew their strength; they shall mount up with wings as eagles, they shall run, and not be weary; and they shall walk, and not faint. (Isaiah 40:28-31)

Two Sets of Muscles

An Army Drill Sergeant trains young men in a most difficult manner. Just a few days before they could not make a bed, carry out the garbage, mow the lawn, pick up their clothes, or wash behind their ears without their mother standing over them. Suddenly, these same young men are clean shaven, able to make a bed that bounces a quarter, glad to march all day and even able to make a twenty-five (25) mile hike carrying a weapon and full gear. What was the change? It was the development of a winning attitude. It was the awareness that they were part of a team. Knowing that others depended on them made them keep going. They developed this confident attitude partially because the Drill Sergeant understood that they had walking muscles and running muscles. On a long march, the Sergeant walked them until they were about to fall, then he ordered, "Double time, March!" Now they must go twice as fast as before. They couldn't stop; they must try. Surprisingly, their legs worked and now they are marching double time (180 steps a minute) even though they were about to fall at (90 steps a minute). What was the difference?

Humans have walking muscles and running muscles. While they were marching, their running muscles were at rest. Now, at the double time, their walking muscles are resting. About the time the running muscles are getting fatigued, the mean old Sergeant, gives an order to return to the regular march cadence. Again, the young men are surprised that they can continue. They actually feel refreshed. Their confidence grows. They realize they are young and strong and can win in battle.

After a short rest at the half way mark, the Sergeant says something like this, "It's just 12 miles to camp. If we hurry we can make chow!" They are ready. By the time they reach camp, they are a fighting team with an overcoming attitude. Scripture suggests that believers can run and not grow weary, walk and not faint. Have you developed this capacity? Have you used all your muscles? Are you willing to persevere until all your private demons are vanquished?

Two Kinds of Knowledge

There are two kinds of knowledge: natural physical information made up of facts, which are actually happening in the physical arena, and spiritual "truth", which is a special kind of knowledge based on facts in Scripture and faith. In fact, facts or information when tried by the Spirit and common sense, become spiritual knowledge. This knowledge supersedes, overpowers, and consumes the physical arena. Victory comes from spiritual truth and right action. This can be illustrated by the story of the two buckets.

Two Buckets

One bucket was an optimist and one was a pessimist. They illustrate a great truth. The empty bucket, the pessimist approached the well and said, "I never come away from the well full but that I return again empty." The pessimist saw life as a disappointing event. The optimists bucket said as it left the well full of water, "I never come to the well empty but that I go away full."

Accentuating the positive and eliminating the negative is the only way to develop the attitude that overcomes.

> 1. Now faith is the reality of things being hoped for, the proof of things not being seen. 6. It is impossible to please God without faith. No one reaches God's presence until he has learned to believe that God exists, and that God is one who rewards those who are seeking him out.(Hebrews 11:1,6 EDNT)
>
> 6. But let him ask in faith, nothing wavering, for he that shows doubt or indecision is like a wave of the sea driven with the wind and tossed. (James 1:6 EDNT)
>
> 9. Be strong in faith and stand up to the devil, knowing that you share the same suffering with your brothers all over the world. (1 Peter 5:9 EDNT)

Two Houses

A real estate agent shows a young couple two houses. They are identical. Except for the neighborhood, the floor plan, the color, every aspect of the houses were identical. One house sits at the end of a long dark, lonely street in an unkempt neighborhood. The other house is situated in a bright, open area flooded with sunshine and colorful foliage in a well cared for community. Which of these two houses do you think the young couple would choose as a home, as an environment for their children, as a place for restful sleep? It is the surrounding atmosphere, not the houses, that influences the couple's decision.

Christian Lifestyle

The same is true when it comes to your Christian lifestyle. Your conviction toward obedience to God and resistance toward Satan is the atmosphere that surrounds you. It is this environment that creates a positive mind set toward obedience. Each of life's situations is influenced by your decisions. Attitude is your mental state, your posture, your position as a person, your emotional mood, your general disposition, and the expression of your opinion. Your viewpoint as a Christian might be called your spiritual aura. If it is positive, you will resist the evil and embrace the good. A distinct atmosphere of obedience should surround you as a representative of Jesus Christ.

Speaker of the Present

Your attitude says more about you than does your words. You may try to mask true feelings, but you will rarely succeed. The roots of inward thoughts normally express themselves in outward fruit or behavior. You may pretend that everything is all right, but since your perception is an outward look based on your past experience, you will soon reveal your true feelings. Your true attitude becomes the speaker of the present. It cannot be concealed. Sin will be revealed. Evil deeds done in the closet will be shouted from the rooftops. You are certain that consequences to wrong behavior exist. Learn the lesson of Saul: obedience is better than any sacrifice.

Demeanor is a Prophet

Demeanor is also a prophet of the future. Action is a measurable predisposition of an inward attitude. When looking at your state of mind and behavior under certain circumstances, your attitude becomes the prophet and predicts the way you will respond in the future. In other words, if you permit Satan to defeat you in little things, he will overcome you in the important battles of your life. Every root of bitterness, every inclination toward evil, must be conquered and vanquished from your life. The way you behave now will become a predictor - a prophet

- of what your behavior will be in the future. Will you storm the ramparts? Will you resist evil until every foe is vanquished?

The Language of "Poor Me"

Few leaders of early Christianity had greater difficulty than the Apostle Paul. Whether Paul was in prison, drifting in the sea or being persecuted as a Christian, he never used the language of "poor me". He seemed to appropriate the mind of Christ and constantly adjust his attitude for the better. Under the most extreme circumstances Paul looked to the future with confidence. On one occasion when Paul and Silas were in prison at midnight, instead of holding grudges or holding a pity party, they prayed and sang praises to God. They permitted their faith and their relationship with Christ to storm the ramparts of evil and overcome the forces that would drag them down to despair. They prayed and sang until the evil forces were vanquished and the jail was opened and they were again in the fresh air of faith.

> 25. At midnight Paul and Silas prayed and sang praises to God: and the prisoners heard them. 26. Suddenly there was a violent earthquake that shook the foundations of the prison: and at once all the doors were opened and everyone's bands were loosed. 27. And the jailor was startled out of sleep and seeing the prison doors open, drew his sword to kill himself thinking the prisoners had all fled. 28. But Paul shouted out, Do yourself no harm: for we are all here. 29. Calling for a light, the jailor rushed in and fell trembling at the feet of Paul and Silas, 30. and leading them outside said, Sirs, what is necessary for me to be saved? 31. And they said, Believe on the Lord Jesus Christ and you and your house shall be saved. 32. And they explained to him the word of the Lord and to all that were in his house. 33. And he took them the same hour of the night and washed their stripes; and he and his household were baptized without delay. 34. And he

brought them to his house and set food before them and rejoiced, believing in God with his whole house. (Acts 16:25-34 EDNT)

A Man of Faith

Paul was a man of faith. He claimed that faith put him right with God and that he enjoyed peace with God through Christ and had been brought by faith into the very experience of God's grace in which he presently lived. Paul was excited about sharing the glory of Christ; he also was not troubled because he would endure the tribulations and afflictions that would come to him as a believer. He truly believed that these tribulations would work steadfastness and bring about perseverance in his life and that it would produce an overcoming spirit, a spirit of hope.

> 18. For I consider the sufferings we now endure not worthy to be compared with the glory about to be revealed in us. (Romans 8:18 EDNT)

It was this hope that made Paul an overcomer. The Bible is clear that we cannot have it both ways. We cannot be double minded and unstable to the point of spiritual vacillation.

> 8. A two-spirited man is unsettled and wavering in all his direction, position or manner. (James 1:8 EDNT)

Just as you cannot go in two directions at once, you cannot go up and down at the same time. You cannot have the mind of Christ while permitting your own will to control you. The battle will not be won unless you have confidence in the outcome. You must bring your whole personality, your mind, your will, your emotions, and your psyche under the control of the Spirit. You must not allow the enemy to dictate to you how you are going to live or what your life will be. Let your outward expressions become true windows of your soul. Be happy and rejoice in the circumstances that God has made. Resist Satan and be an overcomer.

Smith Wigglesworth

A powerful preacher by the name of Smith Wigglesworth said to some friends, "I'm not moved by what I see, I'm not moved by what I feel, I'm moved by what I believe." When we permit what we believe to control our actions, these actions can change the outcome of life's battles and we can win. No adversity, no perplexity, no confusion can overcome the believer who truly submits to God and resists Satan. This is what it means to be an overcomer!

Why should we live miserable lives? Why should we waste valuable seconds of our lives worrying about the outcome of life's battles? To worry is to take responsibility for something that belongs to God. Turn over to the back of the Bible and read the ending: the good people win. Believers must not look at the mountain or the darkness. They must not see the perplexities or the problems. Circumstances of life must not control your attitude. Subdue the tendency to complain, to find fault, to make accusation, to blame. Let the power of love refresh your spirit. Resist evil until every foe in your life is vanquished.

Attitude is Contagious

This attitude is contagious. All of us have seen the small football team, behind in the score but ahead in heart. And we have seen that struggling team score and renew the hope of winning, and against all odds prevail. This is only the prevailing of the human spirit. Now when we add the power of the Holy Spirit, the recreated spirit within the believer, great spiritual victory can be yours. You can storm the ramparts till every foe is vanquished.

A doubting spirit is a dreaded disease that causes a closed mind and a dark future. Doubts are also contagious. When your attitude is positive it is conducive to growth, the mind expands and progress begins. Remember that life is a temporary situation. It is constantly changing. Things that are eternal or of the spirit are controlled by supernatural power. Submit yourself to God; resist evil. The enemy is a vanquished foe.

Check the Moustache

Then there is the story about the grandpa who was taking an afternoon nap. The visiting grandchildren decided to play a joke on their grandfather. So while he slept, they rubbed some Limburger cheese in his moustache. As the aroma of the cheese penetrated his handlebar moustache and began to awaken him, the children hid. As the grandfather was awakened by the startling smell, he began to sniff around the room, "This room stinks," he declared. The children were having a ball. As grandpa moved through the house he would say, "This whole house stinks." Finally, he went outside to get a breath of fresh air and he decided, "The whole world stinks." Well, it was just grandpa's moustache, and once he discovered it, the problem was easily corrected.

Things are wrong with the world. Everything may not be totally right even within the local congregation, but before you begin to accuse and condemn perhaps you should check your own moustache. Perhaps you can change the world, even your local congregation, by changing your own moustache. An honest recognition of personal faults can create an atmosphere that is conducive to improvement, and by adjusting your attitude, the circumstances of life can be changed for the better. You can resist evil and do better. This is done by being submissive to God

7. Be God's true subjects; stand firm against the devil, and he will vanish from you. 8. Bow down before God, and He will be near your hand. You who have erred and missed the mark must cleanse your hands, and you who have wavered or are two-spirited must free your thoughts and feelings from guilt. (James 4:7,8 EDNT)

Subordinate your Will

To be submissive to God; that is, subordinate your will to the divine will, and be under complete obedience. One should never seek to resist the devil without first assuring their submission to the Lordship of Christ and the perfect will of God. This includes drawing near to God, purging clean one's personal life, and sanctifying or making clean the heart. The process requires a humbling before the Lord. Then God will lift up the believer much as God did Israel. When the believer waits on the Lord their strength is renewed. They fly with the wings of an eagle. They persist on the journey.

The overcoming attitude is one that perseveres. Coaches in high school are able to develop such an attitude in young athletes. The runner is told, "If you don't win, the fellow who beats you better break a record." The players are told to never give up, don't quit. Young players stay in the game with injuries that should hospitalize them, but their will to persevere is so strong they continue.

An Overcoming Attitude

An overcoming attitude prompts action. Action changes ones attitude about the outcome of the battle. With action one is ready to take advantage of opportunities. In fact, to the believer, opportunity equals obligation. "As we have therefore opportunity, let us do good to all men."

> 10. As we have opportunity, let us practice generosity to all, especially to those who are of the congregation of faith. (Galatians 6:10 EDNT)

> 10. But I rejoiced greatly in the Lord that at last your care of me has flourished again; wherein you were also concerned, but lacked opportunity. (Philippians 4:10 EDNT)

When opportunity comes, God will prompt our action. Beware the sin of omission! When one knows to do good, but chooses not to act; it is sin. The sin of omission can handicap an individual and bring personal defeat in their spiritual battles. This is why each one needs the care and comfort of a local congregation and the fellowship of believers to serve as a bulwark against failure. Individuals may fail. Spiritual leaders may be defeated. Even Nations shall fail, but God's word shall never fail. As long as God's Word prevails, Christianity shall prevail. The very gates of hell cannot prevail against God's Kingdom. The fellowship of believers is a bulwark never failing and an instrument of God for world evangelism.

> 1. My son, keep empowering yourself in the grace that is in Christ Jesus. 2. And entrust the things you learned from me which were confirmed by many witnesses, to faithful men who will be competent to teach others also. 3. Join the ranks of those who share hardships as a soldier of Jesus Christ. 4. No active warrior entangles himself with ordinary affairs; so he may please the one who enlisted him as a soldier. (2 Timothy 2:1-4 EDNT)

CHAPTER EIGHT

A Bulwark Never Failing

> Did we in our own strength confide,
> Our striving would be losing,
> Were not the right man on our side,
> The man of God's own choosing.
> Dost ask who that may be?
> Christ Jesus, it is He-
> Lord Saboeth is His name,
> From age to age the same
> And He must win the battle.
>
> - Martin Luther -

Where are the Heroes?

In the Book of Hebrews there is a list of Heroes of the Faith. They were not presented in any particular order, but the outstanding characteristics of each are mentioned. The victories are bound together by a simple act of faith and divine intervention. Look at the list:

> 32. And what more shall I say? Time will fail me to recount the story of Gideon, Barak, Samson, Jephthah, David, Samuel and of the prophets, 33. men who, through faith, mastered kingdoms, did righteousness, obtained promises, shut the mouths of lions. 34. Quenched the power of fire, escaped the edge of the sword, in their weakness they were made strong, showed courage in battle, made foreign armies yield. (Hebrews 11:32-34 EDNT)

Gideon – with only 300 men won a victory over overwhelming odds against people who had terrorized Israel, a victory that still is a source of encouragement in the spiritual warfare.

Barak – under guidance of prophetess Deborah, Barak assembled 10,000 men and faced 900 war chariots ofiron to win an incredible victory. It was similar to a band of light infantry routing a division of tanks.

Sampson – always worked alone with only his physical strength; always faced amazing odds and emerged triumphant. Sampson in this isolation using his faith and strength became a scourge of the enemies of Israel.

Jephthah – was an illegitimate son driven into exile, but when his military skills were needed by Israel this forgotten outlaw was called back into service and won a tremendous victory.

David – a shepherd lad anointed king over his brothers led Israel to great victories over many enemies.

Samuel – born late in life to a praying mother became a faithful man of God in the midst of a frightened, discontented and rebellious people.

Prophets – man after man became faithful witnesses of God's power. These were the men who faced incredible odds and believed God was on their side against all enemies. In human terms they faced impossible God-given tasks and achieved victories. These were men who were never afraid to stand alone and face immense odds and achieve victory with divine assistance. Where are such men today? Are there no prophets in the land that can stand up for morality, ethics, fairness and the unalienable rights of Christians to worship and practice their faith in the marketplace?

The last part of these verses (Hebrews 11:32-34) tells of these and others who made spiritual impact during their life. The writer uses phases that in the original language are more reveling than in the English translation. The word used for mastering kingdoms is the same that Josephus used for David's exploits. Wrought righteousness is the Old Testament term used in describing David as a leader. Stopping the mouths of lions relates to Daniel. The phrase quenching the violence of fire refers to the three Hebrews placed in the over-heated furnace because they would not bow to a god other than Jehovah. Escaping the edge of the sword refers to Elijah and others threatened with assassination. Strong in warfare and routing the ranks of the aliens speaks of many brave warriors who won battles against superior enemies to achieve victory for God's people.

Saints Triumphant

One summer during Vacation Bible School the teacher was leading the children in singing, "If you are saved and you know it, say Amen!" One little blonde about eight years old sang to the top of her voice: "If you are SAFE and you know it...." The teacher tried to correct the girl, but to know avail. She had never been lost in the woods or at the shopping mall, she had no concept of "lostness;" therefore, "saved" had no relevance to her young life. However, her big brother played in the Little League and she understood what it meant to be "safe" on first base and safe at home plate. Afterwards I looked up the word "saved" in the dictionary and was surprised to learn that the girl was right: it meant, *"safe; to make safe; to be put in safety."* The young girl knew the feeling of safety. She felt secure in her home, at school, at church, and in the community. Christians are supposed to feel "safe" and secure in the fellowship of other believers. All believers should have a triumphant attitude. We are not only safe in the arms of Jesus, we are saved from the wrath to come. We are Saints Triumphant! Through a conquering Christ, we shall be victorious. The daily battles will be won. The campaign against spiritual darkness will be enlightened by the witness of our faith. We shall overcome and be triumphant in the global war against the moral weakness that threatens the roots of our society.

The Family of God

To be born again is to become a part of the family of God, the First Family. This is a position of honor and safety. "The angels of the Lord encampeth round about them that fear him, and delivereth them." (Psalm 34:7) With the assurance provided by the personal pronouns in Psalms 23, each believer should feel safe in the arms of Jesus and secure within the bulwark of saints. The worship sanctuary should be a safe place where one feels protected.

This sense of sanctuary includes both the preservation of a secure state, and also the rescue, deliverance and restoration of anyone who goes astray. Consequently, the believer should have no fear, but simply resist evil and be encouraged by the confidence that comes from the knowledge of being in the family of God. The assurance that nothing can separate the unwavering believer from the love and protection of the father is strengthened by the knowledge that one may be in the family of God and dwell in the house of the Lord forever. Should the believer become discouraged and fall into temptation, the spiritual leadership is there to restore. "Where no counsel is, the people fall: but in the multitude of counselors there is safety." (Proverbs 11:14) As believers stand together and form a network of mutual support, the fellowship becomes a strong bulwark against the enemy. This care of souls becomes a cure for souls and a strong method of continuance that guarantees the viability of the congregation in spiritual warfare.

God's Hedge

Deep in the Old Testament is an account of God's protection for the righteous. It seems that God had built a hedge about Job and his possessions and Satan could not break through to tempt Job. "Hast not thou made a hedge about him, and about his house, and about all that he hath on every side? (Job 1:10) The word for "hedge" here included being shut in for fortification, protection, or restraint. God's hedge was a fence to keep the devil outside and Job inside. If that were true, even before the Age of Grace, how much more will God protect His own now in the final days before Christ's return?

Satan is not omnipresent, he must go to and fro in the earth, but God is everywhere. Satan had to ask God to remove the protective hedge from about Job. God's purpose in allowing Job to be tested was to purify and strengthen his faith. It worked. Job overcame and was victorious in every respect. In fact, Job had a double portion of everything after he joined the ranks of the overcomers. If there were no battles, one would never understand victory. If there were no sickness, one would not know the value of health. Even light is defined by the absence of darkness. The good is often known and understood in contrast with the bad.

Shut in with God

Once I heard an old preacher sing, *Shut in with God*, and it impressed me sufficiently to change my prayer life. The author is unknown to me, but he must have been a praying man.

>Chorus: Shut in with God in a secret place
>There in the spirit, beholding His face
>Gaining new power to run in this race
>Oh, I love to be shut in with God.

Blood washed believers are hid with Christ in God and sealed by the Holy Spirit. Satan cannot cross the blood line. There is security in salvation; full assurance comes when one clearly understands their position in Christ.

> 3. You have already undergone death and your new life is hid with Christ in God. (Colossians 3:3 EDNT)

> 13. In whom you also trusted, after you heard the word of truth, the gospel of your salvation: in whom after you believed, you were sealed with the Holy Spirit of promise, 14. which is the first installment until the full redemption of the purchased possession, to His praise and glory. (Ephesians 1:13 EDNT)

Alliance of Believers

To maintain security and resist the inroads of immorality in Christian institutions, all believers should commit themselves to a local congregation and join forces with kindred minds. To truly resist evil one must be joined in heart with those who want to resist Satan. There needs to be agreement to be effective in spiritual warfare. All must be involved in developing a defense strategy. A house divided against itself cannot resist the attacks of evil. To be of one mind, one accord, in one place brings strength and power to the group. Agreement and unity are vital to an effective defense strategy. To adequately resist Satan, believers must be joined with kindred minds ready to resist all who would attack the congregation and its role in the community.

An Effective Defense Strategy

The local congregation by its essential character, should be a group of kindred minds concerned about one another and the community in which they live. To mount an aggressive defense with sufficient numbers to make a significant difference, the gathered church should see the worship sanctuary as a place of shelter and refuge to be defended by all.

In the old city-state era of history, only men of property were called to defend the walls of the city against attackers. The reasoning was that property owners would be more aggressive in the protection of their own property. Each member of the local congregation has a personal stake in the ongoing ministry and survivability of the Christian movement. This makes a powerful difference, because both men and women, young and old, new converts and mature saints can join hearts and defend the cause against evil.

Numbers and Spiritual Arithmetic

Two cannot walk together unless they are in agreement (Amos 3:3). According to Solomon it is dangerous to travel life's journey alone, because there are times in life when everyone needs assistance. The common 911 call, "I have fallen and can't get up!" also speaks to the spiritual. The strong must help the weak. Believers must bear one another's burdens, but one should remember that numbers alone are not sufficient. There has to be a commitment to one another and a willingness to come to another's rescue. The scripture "For where two or three are gathered together in my name, there am I in the midst of them," (Matthew 18:25) speaks to more than numbers: the operative concept is togetherness.

There must be a spiritual togetherness, kindred minds joined in heart, and the gathering must be in the Name of Jesus. When these dynamics exist, it is more than numbers; the gathering is filled with the power of Christ and this compounds the numbers and some special arithmetic begins to fortify believers. Moses explains the spiritual arithmetic to Israel: How one could chase a thousand and two put ten thousand to flight.

(Deuteronomy 32:30) The strength of character and commitment to God makes for a powerful combination in developing a strategy of resistance against evil.

Building the Wall

When the walls of Jerusalem were rebuilt to restore the integrity of the Name of God, the people worked on the wall nearest their house. There was opposition from outside forces, so they held a weapon in one hand and worked with the other. The people were encouraged to work and not fear the enemy. "Be not afraid of them: remember the Lord, which is great and terrible, and fight for your brethren, your sons, and your daughters, your wives, and your houses." (Nehemiah 4:14) They were separated working on different parts of the wall, but there was an emergency plan. "In what place therefore ye hear the sound of the trumpet, resort ye thither unto us: our God shall fight for us." (4:20) God expects His people to work and resist Satan, and he will fight the battle. The battle is the Lord's.

A Shining City on a Hill

Early in Christian history, believers built the church buildings on a hill with a steeple pointing to the sky for all to see. They did not hide the light of the gospel. The church building was often the most fortified place in the community and during trouble the families took refuge in the building as a sanctuary. God wants His "church" to be fortified against evil and ready to defend the faith once delivered to the saints. The local congregation should be a city of lights, filled with burning hearts and shining testimonies, ready to knock holes in the darkness of this world.

The Winning Side

The human element may fail, but God's church will

never fail. The gates of hell shall not prevail against the church of the living God. (Matthew 16:18) Trouble comes and difficulties arise, but the institution called "church" will survive. I have turned over to the back of the good book and found out the final outcome. We are on the winning side! God and His Kingdom will prevail.

Christ's Return

Luke speaking of the last days, said that men's hearts would fail them fro fear, and for looking after those things which are coming on the earth.

> 25. And there shall be mysterious indications in the sun, moon, and stars: and on earth the nations shall feel hopelessness and bewilderment by the roaring of the sea; 26. men's hearts will panic for the anticipated horror coming on the earth: and the heavens shall be powerfully shaken. 27. And then shall they see the Son of Man coming with full power and grandeur. (Luke 21:25-27 EDNT)

Paul spoke of the suffering of believers and the anticipated glory of God's revelation.

> 18. For I consider the sufferings we now endure not worthy to be compared with the glory about to be revealed in us. (Romans 8:18 EDNT)

We are on the winning side, but the battle is not over. We must look to the local congregation as a bulwark against the onslaughts of Satan. We must persevere... preach, teach, and resist evil until Christ comes in glory.

Will He find Faith

When Christ returns, will He find faith on the earth? Yes, because we are going to stand in the gap and pray and give the next generation a chance to receive Christ and live in this present evil world as Christians. The church will be triumphant. Though Satan may come in like a flood, God shall raise both a Standard and a Christian Army against him. The forces of hell will not prevail. For each and every believer and for the seeking sinner, the local congregation must be a bulwark that never fails. The Revelation of Jesus Christ is the last word. The overcomers are on the winning side! Thanks be to God who gives the victory!

The Last Word

> 19. As many as I love, I correct and chasten: be zealous therefore, and repent. I am standing at the Door. 20. Behold, I am standing at the door, and continue knocking: if any man listens to My voice, and opens the door, I will come in to him, and will feast with him, and he with Me. 21. To him who overcomes will I grant to sit beside Me in My throne, even as I also overcame, and am set down beside My Father on His throne. 22. He who has an ear let him listen to what the Spirit says to the churches. (Revelation 3:19-22 EDNT)

We must take courage and find a new sense of responsibility. This can be done by remembering all the great things God has done for His People through the years. History is His-Story! God's victories are recorded in sacred Scripture. Should discouragement overtake us, we must look to the Captain of our Salvation and follow His commands. The God who gave Israel victory after victory is still willing and able to assist us in the fight. His arm has not been shortened, nor has His ear become heavy. What God did for others He will do for us. What God did once, He will do again. He is the God of History; the God of Victory: the same God we worship daily.

To digress to a secular example: Napoleon was not a religious man, but he was a great general. Scripture reminds us that at times "men in darkness are wiser than children of the light." Napoleon once said, "In every battle there comes a time when both sides have lost; the side that attacks first after that point will win the battle." Provided we join forces with a spiritual strategy and act openly and responsibly, and attack the enemy on his turf we shall overcome the moral corruptness in the world. We must fight the good fight of Faith and lay hold on eternal life. The true universal church will be triumphant. I have already turned to the last pages of the Good Book: believers are on the winning side. Let us together claim the victory. We are on the winning side and nothing can withhold victory from saints triumphant!

> 10. Finally, my brothers, be strengthened in the Lord, and in the power of His unlimited resource. 11. Wear the complete armor of God, so you can stand against the strategy and assault of the adversary. 12.For our wrestling is not against a physical enemy, but against evil princes of darkness who rule this world, against hosts of spiritual wickedness in heavenly warfare. 13. Wherefore wear the complete armor of God that you may be able to withstand evil attacks when they come, and be found still standing. 14. Stand your ground, being protected by Truth, and having integrity for a breastplate; 15. and the gospel of peace preparing your feet for battle, 16. above all, take the shield of faith to extinguish all the fiery darts of the wicked. 17. And take the helmet, which is salvation, and the sword of the Spirit, which is the word of God: 18. praying on every occasion through petition in the Spirit, and be vigilant with unwearied perseverance and supplication for all saints; 19. and pray for me, that fluency of speech may be given me, that I may make known courageously the sacred secret of the gospel, 20. for which I am an envoy in a coupling-chain bound to a guard: that in spite of that detail I may speak bravely, as I ought to speak. (Ephesians 6:10-20 EDNT)

Afterword

Audacity and Spiritual Courage

After attending the Air Force War College, I was sent to Vietnam during the Tet Offensive (1968) as a Reserve Chaplain to do research on the wartime activity of chaplains. Unless a person has been shot at in a combat zone, they have little knowledge of warfare. After this sojourn, I began a serious study of Dietrich Bonhoeffer and his resistance to Hitler during World War II. He was a true "witness" in faith and action, and surrendered his life to complete resistance to the Nazi Regime. His wartime activity ultimately brought about his execution at the hands of the Gestapo. Have you resisted evil forces that would dominate the world? Are you ready to continue the fight against the Amalekites that war against God's people? Are you willing to fight against all forms of evil in society? Perhaps a few words about Bonhoeffer would encourage the faint of heart.

Audacity and Spiritual Courage

During the build up to WWII, Hitler and the Third Reich in their opposition to Judaism attempted to control all religions and bring the German church under Nazi supervision. Dietrich Bonhoeffer demonstrated fearless courage in his personal resistance to the Nazi government. Courageous wartime activities initiated the process that led to his execution. Through the Confessing Church, which resisted governmental infringement, Bonhoeffer began to develop the concepts of principled responsibility in relation to the spiritual life. During his imprisonment, he worked further on a personalized approach to discipleship.

Bonhoeffer expressed a different perspective on life and religion in his prison letters. It took real courage to live the disciplined life during wartime, but perhaps it takes more audacity and spiritual courage to resist the creeping secular influence on the faith-based community in times of peace. Silently, secularism has encroached on the nature of marriage, abortion issues, the subject of death and dying, and the moral fiber of individuals. The faith-based community must resist all encroachment on religious and personal liberty.

An Antecedent Obligation

Although Bonhoeffer made fragmentary suggestions about a time when there would be no religious influence in world affairs, his statements concerned the reality of faith, not the formal, public expression of religion. He believed that Christianity had an antecedent obligation that binds believers as a social force to certain responsibility. He suggested that the meanness of war had annihilated this viable historical possibility of moral resistance against evil.

Looking at the tragedy of war, Bonhoeffer understood that preaching and teaching of the German church did not create a human conscience to prevent the inhumanity of armed conflict during the decades of two world wars. The wartime conflict crushed the internal principles by which Germany engaged the world and the men who committed wartime atrocities had been under the influence of the German church for decades. The tragedy, according to Bonhoeffer, was that the church seemed to have no influence on the social policies of the government or the behavior of the German soldier. This left the soldiers of the Third Reich with no moral grounding and enabled them to behave in an uncivilized manner against the Jewish people, the poor, the homeless, the disenfranchised, and anyone who did not look or speak exactly as they did. What does this say about the current state of Christianity?

Personalized Faith without old Presuppositions

Bonhoeffer in his earliest mention of a new "religionless world" (30 April 1944) suggested that men in the future would speak of God in a secular manner rather than as informed theologians. He not only raised the possibility of different means of expressing religious language, but that it would be without the old presuppositions and institutional aspects of the state church. He pointed to a time when believers would return to the individual level of faith and practice based on biblical principles rather than the organized format that persists in Western culture.

Perhaps organized religion will continue its crippled performance of playing church, the second front of missionary outreach will be allowed to waste vital resources through defective efforts, and the ineffective guerilla-type operation of unprepared individuals functioning on foreign soil, digging wells, planting corn, and teaching carpentry, will be lauded as a religious "peace corps." This is good community service, but it lacks the aggressive militancy needed to destroy the evil Amalekites. This is happening while the marketplace of the work-a-day world and billions around the globe are lacking the true influence of grace and faith and remain under the power of secular and satanic conduct and practices. Who will go and fight against the Amalekites of the world?

An Adulterated Religiosity

Bonhoeffer's letters pointed to a confidence that "religion" was to be and should be an expression of personal godliness rather than the teachings of an organized church. His writings suggested that the nurturing of the institutionalized religion would not complete an individual's life. This fulfillment would come only by the addition of God through a personal divine encounter. Such an experience could make a difference in the behavior of those who were truly submerged in a faith-based lifestyle that fought against the Amalekites.

This concept conflicts with the pragmatism of modern philosophy that attempts to manipulate human behavior. Such efforts fail to understand the historical reality of the human race; it is consists of individuals. The effort to manipulate does not produce a different person, because the teachings degenerate into a kind of secular religion. Such behavior produces a fatherless fantasy, an adulterated religiosity, and an immoral society. Such individuals will never "fight the good fight" against the Amalekites of the world.

The human race is not free of past religious influence. Modern ideologies have expressed and extended their hold on the population through the institutionalization of religion. The concept that "man had learned to cope with important questions without recourse to God as a working hypothesis" was written by Bonhoeffer's as an original idea (8 June 1944). This construct troubled Bonhoeffer during the final days before his execution at the hands of the Gestapo. He struggled through poetry and letters in a rush to leave a legacy for German believers.

A More Personalized Lifestyle

One day following devotions using Numbers 11:23 and 2 Corinthians 1:20, Bonhoeffer wrote about the promise God gave Moses concerning Divine deliverance. In this devotional mode, he wrote, (21 August 1944) about the believer's "final Amen" and made an appeal for personal Christianity. He postulated that believers must repeatedly immerse themselves in the "life, sayings, deeds, suffering and death of Jesus, to know what God promises and fulfills... again in these turbulent times we lose sight of why it is really worth living." Before Dietrich Bonhoeffer walked out of the concentration camp barracks for the last time, he whispered to a fellow prisoner, "This is the end; for me, the beginning of life." Bonhoeffer was stripped naked and died on a hangman's gallows on the cold morning of April 9, 1945. He was only 39 years old, yet his legacy lives and Germany and the world benefited from his life. His legacy still speaks volumes to those who will listen and follow his example of commitment to a faith-based lifestyle regardless of the cost discipleship. The end was worth the journey. Will you take up the cross of resistance and join the fight against the Amalekites of the world?

Discipleship and Ethics

Individuals, following the example of Bonhoeffer and others, must attack the evils of the present society that threaten the integrity of the faith-based community. The challenge of Bonhoeffer's life and practical theology deals with discipleship and ethics and speaks directly to the present needs of the human race. A willingness to take risks that come from a devotional and principled heart is necessary to capture the spirit of Bonhoeffer. His writings could provide faith-based leadership a perspective about warfare, worship and personal behavior in the midst of conflict. True direction for personal behavior must come from the sacred scripture and the guidance of the Holy Spirit.

Second Front and Guerilla Warfare

A generic least common denominator religion is not

the answer, there must be a re-energized approach to faith-based operations on three fronts:

- fervent local worship groups
- eager "second front" outreach units and
- strategic "guerilla warfare" activity behind the lines to teach the teachable and reach the reachable.

Also, we need more serious prayer groups at home that support the warriors on the front lines of resistance. A moral lifestyle and active witness of faith are essential to this process.

— Hollis L. Green, ThD, PhD

APPENDIX
Spiritual Combat Resources

Christians must develop a strategy of resistance; however, the most potent weapons are personal prayer and the guidance of the Holy Spirit. When believers work together to resist Satan, he is a defeated foe. Satan knows he was defeated at the Cross. When an organized resistance is brought against Satan and his evil cohorts; it must includes all the power of the Cross. We can strengthen the Keepers of the Gate and give the next generation a chance to be Christian. God bless you as you strive to be an overcomer and to lead your community to victory in their spiritual battles.

The listing of these sources and resources should not be considered an affirmation of all the content of the books or the programs of the listed ministries. They seem to be the most studied and referenced material available. Some of the material would be of assistance to those seeking to develop a strategy against the lingering spiritual darkness and the strongholds of Satan that exist in the present world.

Do not discount your own experience and your personal knowledge of the Word of God. Get together with other spiritual leaders in your city. Fast and pray and seek God for guidance in developing a working strategy to resist the onslaughts of Satan against all that is good and wholesome.

Sources and Resources

1. The doctoral dissertation of John David Geib may be purchased from University Microfilm International

(UMI Number: LD03796). He recommends, in particular pages 67-81, (What is Spiritual Mapping?), 177-194 (Responses to Criticisms of Spiritual Mapping) and 220-230 (the actual practices of spiritual mapping).

2. Neil Anderson, *The Bondage Breaker,* Eugene, Ore.: Harvest House, 1990

3. Clinton Arnold, *A3 Crucial Questions about Spiritual Warfare,* Grand Rapids: Baker, 1997

4. John Dawson, *Taking our cities for God: How to break spiritual Strongholds,* Lake Mary, Fla.: Creation House, 1989

5. George Otis Jr... *The Twilight Labyrinth: Why does spiritual darkness linger where it does?* Lynnwood, WA: The Sentinel Group, 1997

6. George Otis Jr... *The Last of the Giants,* Tarrytown, NJ: Chosen, 1991

7. George Otis Jr., *Spiritual Mapping Field Guide, North American Edition*: Lynnwood, WA: The Sentinel Group, 1993

8. Anderson and Mylander, *Setting Your Church Free: A Biblical Plan to Help Your Church,* Ventura, Calif: Regal, 1994

More sources:

John Dawson, *Taking our cities for God: How to break spiritual Strongholds* (Lake Mary, Fla.: Creation House, 1989 and

E. Silvoso, *That none should perish: How to reach entire cities for Christ through prayer evangelism* (Ventura: Calif.: Regal, 1994).

These two are representative core thinking of the spiritual warfare network. Both are sincere believers, and are open to charismatic revelations in addition to Scripture.

Other resources

1) Concerts of Prayer International, PO Box 1399, Wheaton, II. 60189, (708) 690-8441;

2) Mission America, 901 East 78th St., Minneapolis, MN 55420, (612) 853-1762;

3) Christian Information Network, 11025 State Highway 83, Colorado Springs, CO 80921, (719) 522-1040, E-mail 73422.3471@compuserve.com;

4) AD 2000 and Beyond Movement, 2860 South Circle Drive, Suite 2112, Colorado Springs, CO 80906 (719) 576-2000.

Pastors Should Read

Pastors should read the balanced book on Spiritual Warfare *A3 Crucial Questions about Spiritual Warfare@* by Clinton Arnold (Grand Rapids: Baker, 1997). He discusses spiritual mapping in chapter 3 and Otis' views specifically on pages 145, 147-148 and 176.

Another balanced source is Neil Anderson, who heads Freedom in Christ ministries. He has written extensively on individual spiritual warfare *(The Bondage Breaker,* Eugene, Ore.: Harvest House, 1990) and corporate spiritual warfare (Anderson and Mylander, *Setting Your Church Free: A Biblical Plan to Help Your Church,* Ventura, Calif: Regal, 1994). Arnold's *A3 Crucial Questions about Spiritual Warfare@* discusses the seminars that Anderson conducts for churches and cities on pages 190-193.

Pastors who believe they are ministering in a stronghold area could contact George Otis Jr. for resources on Spiritual Mapping at: The Sentinel Group, PO Box 62040, Colorado Springs, 80962. Phone: 719-534-9193; Email: SentinelGp@aol.com.

Otis' book *The Twilight Labyrinth: Why does spiritual darkness linger where it does?* should be read by spiritual leaders if they wish to understand spiritual mapping.

Otis has other resources as well that they may find helpful, and he would probably help them set up a training seminar (as described in a special report from the Sentinel Group on the 1997 International Consultation of Spiritual Mapping titled *To See the World from Heaven's View*.

I leave you with a few lines from the only poem written by my older sister, Mrs. George D. Stout, Sr.

Pray and Push

Pray and push as onward we go,
When is the end no one knows.
When we grow old, as life goes on,
We know pray and push is here to stay.

No one knows when our time is up
To meet our Maker we love so much.
Make me a blessing along the way,
For we are not here to stay.

If we don't knock, the door won't open,
So pray and pray and push until it opens.
Keep the faith and never give up!

And she signed it: "My name is Betty Stout, and I approve this message." (2006)

About The Author

Hollis L. Green, ThD, PhD, is a Clergy-Educator with public relations and business credentials and doctorates in theology, education, and philosophy. A  Distinguished Professor of Education and Social Change at the graduate level for over three decades, Dr. Green is a Diplomate in the Oxford Society of Scholars, and author of 50+ books and numerous articles. He served six years as a member of the U.S. Senate Business Advisory Board and with certified membership in several public relations societies (RPRC, PRSA, and IPRC). He served pastorates in five states, was a denominational official for 18 years, and traveled in ministry and lectured in over 100 countries.

Dr. Green was the founder of Associated Institutional Developers (AID) Ltd., (1974) an international Public Relations and Corporate Consultant Company. He was Vice-President of Luther Rice Seminary (1974-1979), and became the founding President (1981) and Chancellor (1991-2008) of Oxford Graduate School (www.ogs.edu); As part of a global outreach, Dr. Green founded (2002) OASIS UNIVERSITY in Trinidad, W. I. (www.oasisedu.org) where he continues to lecture and teach and assist the administration as Chancellor. In 2004, he assisted in establishing Greenleaf Global Educational Foundation in Colorado to advance issues related to the current needs of society.

In addition to his other endeavors, Dr. Green launched Global Educational Advance, Inc. (2007) to advance higher education and social change through publishing, curriculum development, instruction, library/learning resources, and global book distribution to advance social change. His books and assisting authors in publishing are a logical outgrowth of a sixty-year ministry through education. He serves the Author Publisher Partnership PRESS as Corporate Chair and Co-publisher with his son, Barton. [*www.gea-books.com*] Dr. Green continues to travel, speak, teach, write books, and work with authors in publishing. He maintains a strategy to establish A.I.M (Alpha Institute of Ministry) globally. [*www.globalaim.net*]

A Crowning Achievement

Dr. Green's 42-year project to translate New Testament Greek into a common, devotional language was published in 2014 as a crowning achievement of his ministry.

The EVERGREEN Devotional New Testament EDNT: Complete Edition
>Hardcover ISBN 978-1-935434-28-3;
>Softcover ISBN 978-1-935434-26-9;
>eBook ISBN 978-1-935434-74-0.

Other recent works:

(2014) Research Methods for Problem Solvers
--A Graduate Handbook for Social Research [ISBN 978-1-935434-33-7]

(2014) Fighting the Amalekites (2nd Edition)
--A Guide to Spiritual Warfare [ISBN 978-1-935434-30-6]

(2013) Tear Down These Walls
--Beyond Freeze Frame Thinking and Brand Name Religion [ISBN 9781935434184]

(2013) Remedial and Surrogate Parenting (2nd Ed)
-- A resource for Parents, Teachers, and Childcare Services [ISBN 9781935434481]

(2013) Transformational Leadership in Education (2nd Ed)
--Strengths-based Approach to Change for Administrators, Teachers & Guidance Counselors ISBN 9780980167467]

(2012) SO TALES
--A collection of true anecdotes [ISBN 9781935434580]

(2012) Why Wait till Sunday?
--An Action Approach to Local Evangelism [ISBN 9781935434276]

(2011) Designing Valid Research
--A Brief Study of Research Methodology [ISBN 9781935434573]

(2010) How to Build a Better Spouse Trap
--How to Choose a Mate, Learn from Mistakes, and Stay Married [ISBN 9781935434450]

(2010) Sympathetic Leadership Cybernetics (2nd ED)
--Shepherd Management and Servant Leadership
[ISBN 9781935434528]

(2008) Interpreting an Author's Words
-- Refine Study and Writing Skills [ISBN 9780980167474]

(2007) Why Churches Die
--A Guide to Evangelism and Church Growth [ISBN 9780979601903]

(2007) Why Christianity Fails in America
--Sequel to the American Church Growth Classic Why Churches Die
[ISBN 9780979601910]

(2007) Titanic Lessons
--Do historic realities predict problems for a growing church?
[ISBN 9780979601965]

(2007) Sleepy Town
A Lullaby Song and Story [ISBN 9780979601941]

(2007) Discipleship
--A Vital Aspect of Christian Living [ISBN 9780979601958]

Dr. Green's books may be ordered from

GlobalEdAdvancePress

www.gea-books.com

or anywhere good books are sold.

www.ingramcontent.com/pod-product-compliance
Lightning Source LLC
Chambersburg PA
CBHW021009090426
42738CB00007B/718